WORK AND WORTH
Take Back Your Life

Tony Humphreys
BA, HDE, MA, PhD

Newleaf

Newleaf
an imprint of
Gill & Macmillan Ltd
Hume Avenue, Park West, Dublin 12
with associated companies throughout the world
www.gillmacmillan.ie

© Tony Humphreys 2000
0 7171 3122 X

Design by Vermillion
Print origination by Carole Lynch, Dublin
Printed by ColourBooks Ltd, Dublin

This book is typeset in Rotis Sans Serif 10pt on 13.5pt.

A CIP catalogue record for this book is available from the British Library.

5 4 3 2 1

Inspired by Emily

CONTENTS

WORK: DOES IT MAKE OR BREAK YOU?

Whether you work at home or outside the home, work is an important part of your life. It does not serve anyone when individuals are indifferent to the part work plays in their lives. Work needs to be worthy of your person, dignity, energy and gift-edness. When this ethos is present, workers feel challenged, energised, visible, inspired and satisfied. There exists a healthy flow between their personal, interpersonal, family, recreational, spiritual and occupational lives. Work contributes to their over-all feeling of well-being.

The more common phenomenon is where work either takes over workers' lives or alienates them. When either of these situations is operating, important questions need to be asked and difficult decisions may need to be made.

If you feel work dominates your life, questions that need answer-ing include:

- ☐   Does work make you feel sick?
- ☐   Does work control your life?
- ☐   Does your personal, family and social life suffer?
- ☐   Do you feel your identity is tied up with work?
- ☐   Do you fear failure?
- ☐   Are you addicted to success?
- ☐   Do you live in fear of criticism?

Positive answers to any number of these questions indicate a need for changes in how you see yourself, how you view work and how the work organisation sees you. These are challenges that touch the heart of your personal, family and spiritual security.

If you feel work is demeaning and the workplace is an alien place to be, you need to seriously examine this worrisome situation:

- ☐ Do you feel anonymous in the workplace?
- ☐ Is the work you do worthy and respectful of you?
- ☐ Is the management style aggressive?
- ☐ Is the work culture person or family friendly?
- ☐ Do you shrink from protesting about unfair practices?
- ☐ Do you feel hostile towards work?
- ☐ Does work threaten your sense of self?
- ☐ Do you feel scared in the workplace?

Workers deserve recognition, respect and an empowering style of management. They deserve an ethos that values person and family, allows expression of grievances, is emotionally and socially safe and friendly, and provides opportunities for the development of their unique skills and creativity. Where there is an absence of such care, workers are well advised to take stock of their situation and make decisions that are worthy of their dignity.

It is also the case that work organisations encounter major difficulties with workers who are frequently absent, do the least work for the most money, are hostile, difficult, resentful and undermining of more motivated workers, hate work, fear responsibility and frequently go sick. In an era of high employment and legal restrictions many employers are left floundering, not knowing what to do with workers who are falling short of reasonable expectations or have become a major liability.

Certainly, work organisations benefit from workers who are mature and balanced in their approach to work, but they also gain, in the short term, from those workers who work hard to get everything right with no mind to time or to their personal or interpersonal lives. However, there is a downside to workers who are perfectionistic: they burn out, create difficult staff relationships and make poor leaders.

Like the over-worked or alienated worker, work organisations that are at the receiving end of workers who are either over-responsible or under-responsible need to take strong action to bring about a work environment that generates a fair day's work for a fair day's pay, creates high job satisfaction, provides opportunities for development of giftedness and instils a love of and excitement around work.

PART I

THE POWER OF WORK

'Nothing is more powerful and creative than emptiness –
from which men shrink.'

Chinese sage, Lao-tzu

CHAPTER 1

THE EXPERIENCE OF WORK AND WORTH

THE EXPERIENCE OF WORK

Everybody works. Some people go to jobs; others take care of homes, children, the sick and the elderly; still others do the laundry, clean the house, prepare meals, take care of pets. Each person works at something.

Work is an important aspect of your life and always needs to be worthy of you; it needs also to be deserving of your knowledge, skills, time, energy and dignity. Regrettably, many workers experience not only anonymity but alienation in their places of work. The culture and management style in such organisations can be hostile, overpowering, purely profit focused and lacking in any regard for the personal, interpersonal and family needs of employees. Ironically, these organisations fail to tap into the individuality, creativity and vast potential of workers, and staff morale, motivation to work and productivity suffer greatly from such neglect.

Workplaces consist primarily of two presences: the individual and unique presence of each worker (whether rank-and-file member, manager or employer) and the complex and potentially dynamic group presence of all who operate within the organisation. The interaction between these two presences will largely determine how effective the organisation will be in terms of people and products. Whether employers realise it or not, employees carry their emotional, social, intellectual, religious, sexual and cultural baggage into the workplace. Many employees might have an extremely narrow definition of work, and they might have had a history of work experiences that have led them to hate work or feel threatened by it or get sick at the thought of it or use it as a means of proving themselves. Employers and managers can also possess these protective feelings and attitudes towards work.

Work is the application of the mind and body to tasks aimed at bringing about personal maturity, couple and family harmony, community development and spiritual progress as well as earning a livelihood and being productive in the workplace. In terms of personal development I frequently encourage disenchanted employees to 'work at' being relaxed, quiet, separate from what they do, independent, self-reliant and non-conformist. Most of all I advise them to work at doing nothing. In the quiet and silence of emptiness lies the opportunity to connect deeply with your unique essence, individuality, giftedness and vast power. Many people complain that they find it impossible to still their minds and bodies even for a minute or two. The challenge to do nothing is foreign to them as they have conformed to the notion that to be seen and valued in this world you had better be seen to be doing something. Ironically, it is in the practice of nothingness that you get in touch with your fullness.

An expansive definition of the word 'work' runs contrary to most people's experience. They have come to define work narrowly as applying to domestic, academic, job and career actions. They are well aware of the consequences when they do not 'work hard' at these responsibilities. It is not surprising then that they find the concept of doing nothing the hardest work of all and, indeed, the most emotionally threatening as it runs directly counter to familial and societal expectations. Equally, the invitation to work on self-development is not at all perceived in the same light as the need to work at their jobs or studies. Certainly, in recent years there has been a growing acceptance of therapeutic endeavours, more so for women than for men, but such work is not given nearly the same emphasis as so-called 'more productive types of work'.

Even though work is seen as vital to our progress in life, it is not embraced generally as a wonderful challenge. On the contrary, most people fall into one of three groups: those who are obsessed with work to the point of exhaustion and gross neglect of their personal and interpersonal lives; those who fear and dread going to work; and those who regard work as a chore, a drag, a torment, something to be endured until one can retire. Employers complain that it is difficult to find employees who are honest, conscientious and committed. Many workers are perceived by their employers as 'dossers' doing the least work for the most money. Considerable expenditure is made on implementing stock-control, time-control and financial-control systems to reduce losses through cheating, pilfering, stealing and time wasting. But the same effort is not put into harnessing the potential of these employees. Sadly, many people suffer continuous frustration or intimidation in the workplace. There are those who feel stuck in dead-end jobs and see no hope of change. It is a sad indictment of our culture that such experiences of work are so common. It is short-sighted on the part of educators and employers not to recognise that unless these situations are changed, innovation and productivity will continue to be seriously hampered. A happy, contented worker is far more effective than one who is malcontented.

A further indication of our unhealthy approach to work is that many leading professions — teaching, medicine, nursing, high finance, policing, social work – have become a high health risk but little or nothing is being done to correct this situation. Medical doctors have the highest suicide rate, highest drug addiction rate, highest alcohol addiction rate and highest rate of divorce and family breakdown of any occupational group in modern society. Teaching has become one of the most stressful occupations, resulting in high absenteeism, increasing rates of drop-out from the profession, high incidence of psychosomatic diseases and an unprecedented level of retirement on the basis of ill-health. It is estimated that over 50 per cent of teachers hate their jobs. The toll on teachers' health is now beginning to be measured, but what is not yet being examined is the effects of these teachers on students' attitudes to self, school and work. Children take their cues from the significant adults in their lives – parents, teachers and relatives. Later on as adults they will tend to follow the example of supervisors and managers. When parents, teachers or work leaders exhibit obsessive, fearful or hostile attitudes to work, they are likely to have their charges follow their immature lead. For example, the enthusiasm of many well-motivated young employees is quickly extinguished by a work culture that punishes responsible endeavours.

What is it that keeps people involved in professions that pose so many threats to their physical and emotional health as well as to their marriages and family lives? The simple answer is status, recognition and ambition. But there are deeper underlying issues involved that touch at the very heart of a person's identity and at the deep need for intimacy.

THE EXPERIENCE OF WORTH

When workers are addicted to, fear or hate work, it means that their earlier experiences of work led to a confusion between their individual worth and their work efforts. Children (and adults) deserve to be loved, valued and accepted for their unique person, individuality, differences and giftedness. However, what is more common is that children's behaviours become the determinants of parents, teachers and others demonstrating love to children and withdrawing it, sometimes harshly, when certain behaviours are not present or not executed to a desirable performance level. All infants love to learn and work but the experience of being criticised, ridiculed and rejected because of poor behavioural performance gradually dries up their excitement around challenges. They learn cleverly and quickly to find ways of removing or reducing threats around learning and work. The most common means of reducing possibilities of hurt are perfectionism, avoidance, rebelliousness and sickness.

Sadly, the enmeshment of self with work not only has destroyed the possibility of experiencing work as an exciting and challenging aspect of life but has had disastrous consequences on the emergence of the person's true self. A high proportion of men who retire from work die soon afterwards, even though there was no sign of any physical illness at the time of retirement. I have worked with men who after they retired or were made redundant declared 'There is nothing left in life for me to do' or 'Life has no meaning any more' or 'What's the point in going on?' Not only have these men lost out on the expansiveness of experience — emotional, social, familial, sexual, spiritual, intellectual, physical, political, artistic, creative — but they have no sense of the power and sacredness of their own unique being. The whole of their individual selves and their lives was tunnelled into work, work, work. The enmeshment did not bring them much joy because the tie between self and work became a tight knot of insecurity that squeezed the life blood out of them. Many of these men had lost everything — wife, children, friends, a sense of self, a sense of something greater than self, pleasure, leisure, holidays — for the sake of maintaining identity through work. They may have been successful in terms of career and financial achievement, but there is a hollowness to their victory; having won the battle, they lost the war. Similarly, many women lose their sense of self in the job of homemaker and when children fly the nest their lives are then devoid of meaning and they too are at risk of early death. I have worked with women who subconsciously needed always to have 'a baby in arms' and became deeply threatened when this was no longer possible. I have worked with other women who vehemently tied their adult children to the family of origin, insisting on weekly get-togethers, and any son, daughter or in-law who said 'no' to these arrangements was in danger of being cut off from the 'bosom of the mother'. Nowadays, the most at-risk group of employees is married career women; these women, who are particularly prone to getting cancer, tend to have a double dependence on both career and homemaking as the means of being seen in this world and they literally 'work themselves to death' to maintain high performance levels in both arenas.

Bill Gates, founder of Microsoft and perhaps the leading entrepreneur of the information revolution, says that the greatest impediment to progress in life is success. Addiction to success is like a bottomless vessel that you have to struggle continuously to keep filled, with great costs to all other aspects of your life. When success is your primary goal in life, you have lost sight of your own personal worth and you are driven by the belief that success determines your worthiness.

If success is an impediment to progress, an even greater block is the fear of failure. The fear of failure can sometimes drive people to needing to be always successful, but much more common responses to this fear are avoidance of challenge, going for the average, settling for the minimum, loss of ambition and apathy. Early experiences of failure at home or school, if greeted with harsh criticism, ridicule, scoldings, or humiliating or degrading treatment, lead the child to learn ways of reducing possibilities of failure. There is nothing more devastating for any child, or indeed adult, than to be rejected because of a bit of behaviour. Many employers are puzzled and frustrated by employees who do not show initiative, who do the minimum of work, who lack ambition and drive. What these employers do not see is the wisdom in their employees' strategies. Lowering people's expectations, avoiding risk-taking and not demonstrating creativity — all of these are powerful ways of eliminating possibilities of failure and its embarrassing and rejecting consequences. Unless and until individual employees resolve their fear of failure and the work culture views failure as integral to learning, no amount of either coaxing or harassment is going to remove the blocks to effective and efficient work.

The solution lies in separating self from the experience of work; in so doing you restore self to its unique and sacred place and keep work in its place as one of the many challenging life experiences open to you. This may be a difficult aspiration to achieve on your own. It helps enormously when there exist support groups for this process and even more so when workplaces facilitate and encourage such emancipation. The rewards are great for both the individual and the organisation — independence, high energy, ambition, creativity, increased productivity and job fulfilment.

STEREOTYPING AND WORK

A worrying aspect of contemporary work patterns is that more equal treatment of the sexes is not yet reflected in an equal distribution of males and females across all occupations. The psychological and social occupations — teaching, nursing, social work, psychotherapy, vocational counselling, care work — are predominantly female. The traditionally male-dominated professions – medicine, engineering, architecture, police force, prison officers, science, law — continue to have a greater inflow of males. It would seem that the ghai blue or imposed life roles have not yet been broken. Women are still gravitating towards professions which demand more of the caring and nurturing behaviours that have been considered essential to being female, and men are still drawn to jobs that demand strong, aggressive, ordered and intellectual 'skills' which are typical of the stereotyped male. Even where females have encroached on traditional male occupations — for example banking, politics, law, insurance — managerial staff are still overwhelmingly male.

Much work remains to be done on separating male and female ways of being from feminine and masculine characteristics. Being a male does not have to mean being constrained to masculine-type characteristics and, equally, being a female does not have to entail restriction to feminine-type behaviours. The confusion of masculinity with male and femininity with female has meant that men have largely been cut off from their hearts and confined to their heads, while the opposite is so for women. Whether you are male or female, you have a right to enjoy and experience the full range of human characteristics — feminine and masculine. This is not an issue that can be taken lightly. The fact that most managers are male means that managers often lack the feminine characteristics of sensitivity, empathy, compassion and understanding that are necessary for them to be effective. Males may argue that they possess the masculine traits of firmness and solidity that females tend to lack, but there is no gain in the polarisation of masculine and feminine characteristics. It is the fully rounded person who possesses, for example, firmness and compassion, order and empathy, goal-directedness and warmth, steadfastness and respect who will make the most effective manager.

Another inequality that persists between the sexes is that many males still hold to the belief that their career is more important than that of their female partner. It is still largely the case that the female partner fits her own career development around the male partner's career needs. A related issue is that women are still seen as the homemakers and child rearers.

MARRIAGE, FAMILY AND WORK

From infancy, work affects our lives. Traditionally, father was missing from home from 8 a.m. to 6 p.m. and, in recent years, many mothers have adopted a similar pattern. Where work dominates a parent's life, leading to late homecomings and weekend work, it can have serious effects on family relationships. There is no intention here to suggest that parents should not work outside the home. It is not the quantity but the quality of the time parents spend with children that matters for their children's overall development. It is when parents make work more important than relationships that personal, couple and family problems arise. Furthermore, because children tend to imitate their parents, they too will develop a similar unhealthy focus on work or they may rebel and become apathetic around work.

Parents who run a family business often can have the illusion that because they are around the place they are there for their children and can be shocked when confronted with the reality that mere physical presence is not nearly enough for children (or adults) to feel loved, wanted and secure. Equally, parents who are absent from the home due to overworking can be dismayed when either partner or offspring complain of feeling invisible and unloved. These people believe that 'being the breadwinner' is a means of showing love. Emotional security is a product of the presence of affection, warmth, friendship, affirmation, encouragement, play and social outings. There have to be frequent, sincere and genuine interactions for the formation of relationships and high self-esteem.

Apart from partners or children feeling rejected when work appears to count more than they do, parents' over-focus on work can lead to a situation where the children in turn learn to associate their own sense of self with work. Children will do anything to gain the love of their parents and becoming the 'hard worker' can be a means to getting 'well-earned' attention. The problem is that these children will believe they must always 'be busy' in order to offset any possibility of criticism from their workaholic parents. I have worked with women who will never let their partners 'catch' them sitting having a cup of coffee or leafing through a magazine. They learned this protection at a young age and are now projecting the work expectations of their parents on to their partners. Most people choose a partner who resembles the parent who most influenced them, and if that parent modelled a strong work ethic then this is likely to be reinforced by their partner. I have also worked with men who had huge difficulties in letting go of their role as 'breadwinner' because they dreaded subconsciously that rejection would follow such an action.

It needs to be seen also that parents who dislike or hate work affect their children's attitudes to work and that the couple relationship can suffer too. It would be difficult for a child to show ambition and eagerness to work in the face of a parent who complains constantly about work, comes home tired and irritable, and does not actively encourage them to love work. Neither would such a parent show strong interest in the child's educational development.

Because opposites attract, very often a person who tends to avoid, dislike or do minimal work marries a person who is perfectionistic, highly ambitious or addicted to work. The latter partner can be very critical of the 'malingerer' and vice versa. Disappointment, criticism and conflict can quietly eat into the heart of their relationship. It is very confusing and threatening for children when one parent discounts and the other worships work. Unhealthy coalitions within the family can result from the tension created, with some of the children identifying with and becoming like the parent who finds work a threat to self-esteem and the other children allying themselves with the parent who is addicted to work and following in that parent's perfectionistic footsteps.

It is sad when the worth of a person — child or adult — is seen to lie in behaviour and not in their unique and wonderful being. Depending on the intensity of the work ethic in the home, children can develop major anxiety around work at home and in school. Parents often defend themselves by claiming that they never said verbally to their children they should work so hard, but actions always speak louder than words. It is the parents' own over-involvement with work that children imitate. To be fair to parents, workplaces typically have not been couple or family friendly. Neither have schools been family friendly. Minimal progress has been made in these areas. Society is constantly shouting about the sanctity and value of the family, but it rarely puts its words into action.

Individual adults can certainly address their own attitudes to work and ensure that they see their own person as infinitely more important than their work life and that couple and family relationships vastly outweigh in importance any product. Employers would do well also to create a person- and family-friendly work environment. This process would not mean in any way diluting the responsibilities of employees. It could mean that workers would feel more disposed towards executing their responsibilities. It certainly would bring about an emotionally and physically healthier workforce.

WORK ORGANISATIONS AND WORKERS

It is in the interests of work organisations to appreciate that the level of an employee's or employer's maturity will determine that person's level of work effectiveness. Furthermore, understanding why people work and encouraging them to develop a balanced approach will help both the individual worker and the organisation.

Organisations need also to be aware that the causes of work difficulties may be remote or immediate. Remote causes lie in a worker's earlier experiences of learning and work in the home, school and community. Immediate causes may be due to current problems in the employee's personal and family life or perhaps an exploitative and uncaring workplace. Major conflicts tend to arise from a combination of both remote and immediate causes.

Workplaces are beginning to recognise that it is both an individual and a collective responsibility to develop a work culture and management approach that promotes the welfare of all workers and the organisation. Considerable examination of current work cultures and leadership is needed, and difficult decisions may be required to create caring workplaces. Everyone will gain from such a process and work organisations can be assured that greater dynamism and productivity will ensue. A word of caution is that the development of respect for individual workers must not be conditional on increased productivity. Workers will see quickly the manipulative hand in this and reject it outright. Workers deserve to be valued for their individual selves and not for what they do. I suspect that this is going to be a hard lesson to learn for many entrepreneurs. Unless they develop this unconditional regard for themselves, it is unlikely they will have it for employees. Personal invisibility and anonymity lies at the core of many problems in the workplace.

When work organisations possess a better understanding of the reasons why people work, learn from the work approach of balanced workers, and know how to create a caring work culture and a transformational management style, they can look at ways of preventing problems in the workplace. Prevention is the start-point of effective organisations but, paradoxically, it often follows troubled times.

Organisations that develop preventative and interventionist welfare strategies recognise that though the workplace is difficult and complex, it needs to remain inside the territories of individuality, creativity, feeling and genuine care for workers and the community.

PART II

SELF, WORK AND WORTH

'The greatest impediment to progress is success.'

Bill Gates

CHAPTER 2

WORK AND WORTH

HOW ATTITUDES TO WORK DEVELOP

There is a certain sickness in the Western world which appears to afflict people who are over-ambitious, 'high-flyers', and 'successful' in the popular meaning of that word. These are also the people who, more often than not, become fatigued, anxious, depressed, frustrated, unfulfilled and dependent on medication, alcohol or illicit drugs to handle their weariness and moods. Even though work has become a major block to their emotional, social and spiritual growth, they tenaciously hold on to it. People's attitudes to work vary greatly. There are people who approach their work with passion and zeal; others, even before they leave home to go to work, begin to feel anxious, tense and resentful or fearful and threatened; still others rush forward to work as if going to do battle. How has all this come about? The origins of such attitudes to work are to be found in the first social systems of home and school. The biographical history of a worker, particularly the reactions of parents, teachers and other significant adults to learning and work efforts, hold the explanation of why many people are either addicted to or threatened by work.

The word 'work' is ingrained in our consciousness from early on in childhood and not just from phrases such as 'Daddy is gone to work' or 'Mammy and Daddy have to go to work and the child-minder will look after you until we return.' The word 'work' is employed in multiple ways which signify its importance to the culture that parents, teachers and other adults have adapted to and now wish their children to follow:

- □   'Work hard at your studies.'
- □   'Work your problems out.'
- □   'Work to gain respect.'
- □   'Help your mother with her work.'
- □   'Work your tensions off.'
- □   'Do good works.'
- □   'Your mother and father have to work hard for you.'
- □   'Workaholic.'
- □   'What are you going to work at when you grow up?'
- □   'You have to work for a living.'
- □   'He's a great little worker.'

There are also popular sayings that capture the work ethic prevalent in Western culture:

- □   'Hard work never killed anyone.'
- □   'The devil makes work for idle hands.'

Indirect and implicit references to the importance of work abound in interactions between adults and children and, indeed, between adult and adult:

- □   'What are you sitting there for, doing nothing?'
- □   'You won't go far in this world doing that.'
- □   'What have you being doing all day?'
- □   'What did you do in school today?'
- □   'God loves a trier.'
- □   'Put your back into it.'

The frequent use of the word 'work' stands in marked contrast to the infrequent use of the word 'worth'. As will be seen, a sense of your worth is central to how you live all aspects of your life, and that includes work. When work is sanctified and worth is banished to a largely silent wilderness, it is very difficult for children and adults alike to assert the sacredness and uniqueness of their individual worth.

Whilst words have considerable power in the formation of children's attitudes to work, it is the work behaviours of parents, childminders, teachers, grandparents, relatives and neighbours that have the greatest influence. When children witness a parent devoting excessive time to work and little time to marriage and family, they conclude that work is more important than people and relationships. Once a man in his forties came to me for help to cope with the fact that his wife and children had left him. He complained that 'I worked so hard for them and this is the thanks I get.' What he did not see was that he was addicted to work and spent little or no time with his wife and children. He had married a woman who was opposite to him in her approach to work; she was the 'holidaymaker' and he the 'haymaker'. She was very concerned with pleasure and leisure, experiences that he would not allow himself to pursue. The source of his preoccupation with work lay in his identification with his farmer father. He recalled when he was six years of age being on the tractor with his father and on passing a golf course, his father's words were: 'Look at the crowd of wasters in there, wasting time and wasting good land.' His father worked from sunrise to sundown, never took a holiday and had no leisure interests. As a boy, in order to protect himself from his father's harsh judgment of 'waster', he subconsciously determined that he would be like his father: he would glorify work and denigrate pleasure. Regrettably, the repetition of his father's dependence on work had resulted in the loss of his wife and family. Most children conform to the explicit or implicit expectations of parents and develop attitudes and behaviours similar to parents. When these attitudes and behaviours (whether perfectionistic, avoidant, hostile or apathetic) are strongly reinforced in schools and communities, conformity becomes even more urgent.

As they grow up some children of parents who are over-involved with work rebel, but, unfortunately, they go to the opposite extreme of hating work and not wanting to work. There is wisdom in this seeming madness as these children know full well the emotional vacuum created by work addiction. Nevertheless, their rebellion may result in their missing out on the development of their own creative potential and ostracisation from the majority who may regard them as 'lazy' or 'spoilt' or 'malingerers'. The consequences of such developments are deep unhappiness, depression, no sense of direction in life, frustration, apathy and sometimes aggression. Until their need to be loved by self and for self is resolved, their rebellion against work in itself will not bring contentment.

The word 'work' also applies to unpaid activities within the home, and attitudes towards this kind of work also affect how children will approach work. Women who stay at home and take on the major responsibilities of homemaking can model a work ethic that puts having the home looking perfect before the nurturance needs of themselves, their spouses and their children. I have encountered families where the father complains that 'How the house looks is more important than what myself or the children are feeling.' Similarly, fathers who feel they have to do perfectly whatever activities they take on (for example, gardening, painting, cleaning the car) and who become irritable and moody when things do not go right demonstrate unhealthy attitudes to work. More than likely, such parents carry the same attitudes into the workplace outside the home. There are also parents who will not tolerate their children doing things differently to them and who verbally, non-verbally or physically punish any falling short of their standards. For purposes of emotional survival it becomes expedient for their children to conform to their unrealistic expectations.

Of course there are attitudes to work other than perfectionism that can equally block the development of a love of work. There are parents who for reasons from their own past have learned to hate work or be apathetic around work responsibilities. They often operate from the belief that society owes them something. It would be very emotionally threatening for the children of such parents to run counter to these beliefs, and conformity is a clever means of protecting against rejection. I recall helping a young man who had failed to finish secondary schooling and seemed unable to hold down any job. The apparent reason he was let go from jobs was that he always managed to get it wrong. However, the deeper cause was that his father had no time for work and relied on the state's social security for money for himself and his family. The young man's father gave him no support or encouragement and seemed pleased any time his son lost a job. It took great patience and effort to help the young man to break his enmeshment with his father's lifestyle and forge a more dynamic and responsible one for himself.

The sources of addiction to work, fear and avoidance of work or rebellion against work do not lie totally within the family and school cultures. The prevailing economic climate and the culture of the workplace can either reinforce the attitudes learned in the first social systems that we inhabit or create new blocks to a love of work and to a sense of self-worth. For example, workplaces that are not family friendly, put products before people, have hierarchical power structures, emphasise work performance over realistic and responsible effort and punish failure create an insecure work culture that may foster compensatory, avoidant or rebellious responses. The fact that over 40 per cent of people experience bullying in the workplace is a major source of concern. Research has found that many managers still hold on to the conviction that the only way to get the best out of people is through verbal and sometimes physical aggression. The effects of bullying on the self-esteem of those at the receiving end is well documented.

Clearly the economy of a country, region or locality also affects attitudes to work. Long-term unemployment of workers and poor prospects of work for young people can have profound effects on the motivation to work and one's perception of self.

THE WORLD OF WORTH

As an adult your sense of worth needs to be totally separate from work or any other behaviours or characteristics. Your worth lies in your unique and vastly capable being. When your sense of self is enmeshed with behaviour, you are forced to limit your value and power to the confines of the behaviours that you feel determine your worth. When you believe you have to be successful at work in order to be acceptable to yourself and others, you are imprisoned by the constraints of that dependence.

Furthermore, when you become focused on success as a measure of your worth, anxiety bites at the heels of your power, and your expansiveness becomes narrowed down to the goal of success or the fear of failure. Ironically, when you make progress (personal, interpersonal, career, spiritual) your goal in life and view success and failure as integral to progress, you maintain wonderfully your expansiveness. When you keep your sense of self separate from what you do, you have constant access to your limitless capacity to progress in life. Sadly, there are few of us who allow ourselves direct access to that power. Nelson Mandela expresses this so well in his brilliant observation that 'Our deepest fear is that we are powerful beyond measure.' Most of us have been reared in family, community, school and national cultures that are oppressive and conditional and that reward conformity rather than individuality. Ask yourself the question: 'To whom in the world can I reveal fully and truly who I am, what I think, feel, believe, don't believe, how I behave and know I will be accepted unconditionally?' Most people answer 'nobody' or maybe 'one person' to this question. We live in very unsafe worlds.

Masking your worth and power

The strongest indicators of a strong sense of self-worth are non-conformity, independence of how others regard you, a need for privacy, a love of challenge and a deep respect for self and others. In oppressive relationships and cultures it becomes necessary for individuals to mask their worth and dilute their power, since to show them would threaten the religious, social, educational, occupational and political systems that expect people to be a certain way.

The extent to which your self-worth may be masked ranges on a continuum from low to high. Shadowing of your worth develops in response to the degree of intimidation or over-protectiveness you experience. It is important to see that over-protection of children (and adults) is as crippling of power and worth as are aggression and dominance. The instinctive and wise response to parents, teachers, friends or colleagues who do most everything for you is not to show power, skill and self-reliance because such demonstrations would be read as threatening. The danger would be that those adults you depend on for survival would reject and withdraw from you. Significant adults in your life who do everything for you are insecure; they attempt to control your need of and loyalty to them by making you helpless. This phenomenon is common in many families but it also occurs in the workplace. Masking your worth and power is not a weakness but a clever survival strategy and can manifest itself in a wide range of behaviours, either conformist or rebellious. To be rebellious the person would need to have an ally or allies who would either covertly or overtly support the rebelliousness.

The shadow self

Self-worth refers to your lovability, uniqueness, sacredness and vast capability. Those aspects of you were present at birth and will always be present, no matter how you are treated in this world. A person's being cannot be harmed or damaged, but it can become threatening and even highly dangerous to reveal your true person and power with certain people and in certain places. This is why some people can appear quite self-possessed and confident when they are with people who value them or in subcultures that are respectful of people, and appear inferior and helpless with people who are critical and in places that foster abuse of individuals. What is happening here is a shift in self-esteem depending on whether it is safe or unsafe to be self and powerful. For example, some workers can act quite confidently and competently in the company of fellow workers who respect, like and rely on them, but become timid, unsure and clumsy when faced with a manager who is critical and aggressive. Self-esteem is, then, a shadow self that changes when any threats to your being yourself are present. It is an ingenious protection against being rejected. The greater the threat, the stronger the shadow image projected. Self-worth is a constant and lies behind your defensive clouds. If you feel safe you may test the waters and allow others to catch a glimpse of your awesome being. Individuals who have experienced devastating blocks to being themselves will find it difficult to trust anybody and it may take considerable patience on the part of another to break through their defensive walls. It is a sad indictment of relationships and cultures that people experience more blocks than openness to the expression of their unique being and vast capability. However, it needs to be seen that those people who pose blocks to others expressing their true selves and power are themselves in shadow; their blocking behaviours are their defences against hurt and humiliation. What is happening is that shadow begets shadow, and this cycle will continue until either the perpetrator or the victim begins to find and express their real self. Neglect or abuse is not, then, a cold and deliberate act, but an attempt to protect from further hurt, humiliation and rejection. When blocks exist to the expression of people's true selves, it is the responsibility of all individuals, and the social systems they inhabit, to find ways to break the neglectful cycle.

Blocks to being self can result from either the presence or the absence of certain behaviours. Each block will result in a counter-block so that each party in the relationship or culture is compelled to shadow their light. For example, the colleague of a worker who is highly competitive may counter the threat by attempting to outdo that worker; this reaction may lead to a spiralling of competitiveness and the emergence of serious hostility between the affected parties. The combination of extreme rivalry and aggression shadows the unique worth and giftedness of each of them. Everyone loses out: the conflicting duo, fellow workers who may themselves be drawn into the conflict, and the organisation that has staff members in conflict and showing limited creativity. Listed below are various behaviours whose presence or absence can threaten the expression of self; unless individuals are self-possessed and independent of how others perceive them, some protective response inevitably will emerge in the face of these blocks to being self.

BLOCKS THAT ARISE IN RELATIONSHIPS AND CULTURES

The Presence of:

- ☐ Irritability
- ☐ Hate
- ☐ Distrust
- ☐ Jealousy
- ☐ Competitiveness
- ☐ Violence
- ☐ Sexual abuse
- ☐ Harshness
- ☐ Dominance
- ☐ Control
- ☐ Punishment of failure
- ☐ Over-rewarding of success
- ☐ Passivity
- ☐ Aggression
- ☐ Over-protection
- ☐ Unfair criticism
- ☐ Blaming
- ☐ Denial
- ☐ Ridicule
- ☐ Scolding
- ☐ Cynicism
- ☐ Sarcasm
- ☐ Hostile humour
- ☐ Comparison to another
- ☐ Cruelty
- ☐ Meanness
- ☐ Rigidity
- ☐ Unrealistic expectations
- ☐ Conditional love
- ☐ Labelling (you're 'useless', 'bad', 'no good')
- ☐ Manipulation
- ☐ Threats

The Absence of:

- ☐ Affection
- ☐ Nurturance
- ☐ Recognition
- ☐ Acceptance
- ☐ Understanding
- ☐ Support
- ☐ Compassion
- ☐ Justice
- ☐ Care
- ☐ Responsiveness to needs (physical, emotional, sexual, social, intellectual, creative and spiritual)
- ☐ Opportunities to exercise giftedness and limitless potential

These blocks to the manifestation of self-worth occur in all relationships and in home, school, community, work, religious and national cultures. In the workplace, typical additional blocks are:

- Experience of being 'passed over' for promotion
- Boring, repetitive work
- Redundancy
- Poor working conditions
- Lack of consultation on changes in working conditions or job description
- Lack of appreciation and unjust wages for labour
- Unfair dismissal
- Exposure to a management style that is aggressive, passive or passive-aggressive
- Exposure to an environment that is not person or family friendly
- Purely 'profit' focused
- Experience of bullying
- Lack of back-up systems to deal with neglect
- Long working hours
- No overtime pay
- Lack of hygienic catering and toilet facilities
- Double standards
- Inequality
- Assumptions, values or traditions that are demeaning of workers
- Lack of opportunities to develop skills, exercise responsibility and show vast potential

Experiences that make it difficult to show your power will be perceived in different ways depending on certain factors:

□   *Your level of self-possession at the time:* if you have a strong sense of self you will be less troubled by, for example, unfair criticism than a person who already feels bad about self.

□   *The frequency, intensity and endurance of the blocks:* clearly, the more frequent, intense and enduring are the blocks, the greater will be your protective reactions.

□   *The state of your current physical and psycho-social well-being:* if you are feeling unwell and lacking in energy, or you are in a state of anxiety, depression, hopelessness or despair, or you are delusional or hallucinating, then you are far more vulnerable to further blocks to your sense of your worth.

The shadow protects

It can be seen that the shadow self arises in response to the blocking behaviours of others, particularly the more significant people in our lives: parents, teachers, relatives, close and intimate friends, spouses, work colleagues, managers and employers. Basically what the besieged person learns is that either conformity or rebellion is the means to survive attacks on one's person. The individual who conforms forms a persona, a shadow or screen self, that fits in with the expectations of others. The individual who rebels fashions a shadow self that no one dare approach or contradict. A workplace that is peopled with workers who operate from shadow places is characterised by anonymity, pain, low staff morale, hostility, poor management and decreased productivity.

Light and enlightenment are the most powerful metaphors to express the sacredness, wonder, uniqueness and power of a person. Equally, darkness and shadow have long symbolised a person's invisibility, depression, isolation and hate of self. Cultures too, such as home, school, community, workplace and country, have been described as dark or enlightened. Cultures are the collective life of the shadow behaviours of individuals who people them and the traditions, values, work practices, attitudes, rituals and symbols that over a period of time evolve from the interpersonal blocks to people expressing the light of their worth and power. It is essential to see that though the light may be shadowed, it is never extinguished. On the contrary, the light of self-worth is a constant and lies awaiting behind a person's defensive dark clouds. When the internal or external circumstances are right, the light will shine through and dispel the clouds of anonymity, fear, self-hate, hostility and mediocrity. Furthermore, it is the light that creates the shadow, in the same way that a person who has a unique and precious pearl employs all kinds of safeguard systems to protect it. The creation of the shadow self is a highly intelligent and powerful process and one that will be maintained until it is safe to show your worth and power beyond measure within relationships and places in which you live and work.

It has been pointed out that blocks to people's worth are the defensive behaviours of perpetrators who themselves have encountered threats to their expression of self and power. When people in shadow interact with each other they mutually and automatically block the expression of their true selves. For example, a person who is passive will hide their own individuality and conform to the will of another, who colludes by dominating rather than empowering. The cycle of passivity and dominance will continue until one of them discovers and begins to express their authentic self.

Passivity is not a weakness but a strength against further hurt and rejection. It is an ingenious response to aggression and control, since the absence of confrontation serves the purpose of not increasing the blocking actions of the person who is aggressive. Similarly, fear, timidity and shyness are marvellous protectors. The saying 'once bitten, twice shy' makes tremendous sense. An excessively shy young man once told me that he had been 'bitten' several hundred times by a highly critical and aggressive father and he came to see that his shyness was a formidable weapon against his father's blocking behaviours. People who are shy and timid manage to counter-control others by getting them to back off from them. There are adults that you cannot say 'boo' to without them becoming upset. Who is controlling whom?

Shadow behaviours always have a protective function, and it is the wise parent, teacher, manager or employer who can spot the wisdom of those behaviours and can direct their attention to the light of the real self hiding behind the defensive behaviours. The person who considers the protective responses to be the problem and targets them for change will only bring about an acceleration and a widening of the defensive patterns. Inevitably the individual in shadow will read such manipulation as threatening, controlling and lacking any understanding and will cleverly resort to heightening the defences.

The earlier that protective behaviours begin, the more intricate, complex, compounded and extensive are their nature. When infants and children experience their parents or guardians not celebrating their presence and individuality, they quickly retreat into the shadows. Very often their protective reactions either mirror their parents' blocking behaviours or are diametrically opposed. How often have you been told that you sound and act just like your father or mother or that you are the dead opposite! Either way, you are blocked from progressing in the expression of your true self. When such darkening of their presence is repeated in other social systems (community, church, school), children hold on to their defences. Then, later on as adults, it can take eternal patience and persistence on the part of people who genuinely care for those blocked to help them to let go of their distrust of others.

Your feelings, thoughts, dreams and actions reveal at any one moment whether you are operating out from your real or shadow self. Monitoring of these processes is a first step towards identifying your protective level of self-esteem and taking action to remedy whatever unmet need causes you to keep hidden your true self-worth. Sometimes the change required is to remove yourself from a relationship or particular culture (for example, work or religious) which not only is not affirming but is condemning of your worth. The relationship with self is a key factor in maintaining your wonderful presence and power in the worlds you inhabit (see chapter 7). What also helps enormously is to surround yourself with people who are affirming of your and their own worth and who support you in freeing yourself from your internal and external shadow worlds. Living in cultures that are person and relationship friendly creates further safety for you to be true to self and others.

The responsibility for the emergence of people's true selves must rest not only on the shoulders of individuals but also on home, school, community, church and work cultures. Both individuals and organisations need to be aware that every person hungers for love and recognition, and that material possessions, popularity, fame and job success do not bring peace, contentment, real celebration and joy in living. It is incumbent on work and other social systems to create an environment that celebrates the person and individuality and allows expression of creativity and giftedness. Work organisations need to be person, relationship, family and community friendly and to have managers who are respectful of self and others (see chapters 8 and 9).

Self-worth and personal identity

Self-worth is a given; it is not something you or anybody else creates. Identity refers to the unconscious and conscious process of establishing your difference, initially within the family culture and subsequently with peer groups in school, community and work cultures. An amazing aspect of child development is how each child within a family will find a unique way of expressing self. Even though rarely given credit for such remarkable intelligence, children within a family often act in opposite ways to one another, thereby manifesting their right to have their own identity in this world. When they go to school they may deepen that identity formation or they may adopt a different way of behaving in the school setting. There is, for example, the common phenomenon of the street angel and the house devil. Later on, when peer group becomes an important influence, each child will find a way of standing out through their dress, interests, hobbies, studies, ideals and career choices.

Identity formation is a lifelong process. Some people develop a crystallised identity and remain the same as they were in late adolescence for the entirety of their lives. These individuals tend to be conformist and often repeat the life of one of their parents. Some people experiment with different identities and then eventually develop a recognisable way of being. A small number continue to seek new experiences so that their identity continues to undergo change. These tend to be the more secure and self-possessed group who have the solid base to take on new challenges. Those who operate largely from the shadow self may stick tenaciously to a particular identity or may come to no definite identity. In this way one's sense of self-worth and the process of identity formation are intertwined but they are distinct phenomena. In the occupational world of today, many people may have a minimum of three or four career changes and while this experience is likely to influence their identity development, it does not affect their essential worth.

Confidence and competence

It is common for confidence and competence to be confused with each other. Confidence is knowing and acting on one's vast intellectual and behavioural potential. It is the capability aspect of self-worth and when it is affirmed by significant adults and cultures, individuals stay in touch with their power and do not find challenges threatening. Competence is the development of knowledge and skills. When people believe that it is their level of competence that determines their feelings of confidence, they may have a pseudo-confidence which can be quickly lost when they experience failure.

Belief in us from our parents and the expectations they have of us are the determining factors in the emergence of self-confidence. Complaints of 'He doesn't believe in me' or 'She doesn't trust me' mirror belief difficulties. Complaints of 'He expects too much' or 'She doesn't expect enough' show difficulties around expectations. A clear distinction needs to be made between belief and expectations. Belief in a person is the essential building block of confidence; it is an affirmation of the capability of the person. Expectations need to be addressed to the development of competence and have to do with the encouragement and creation of knowledge and skills. It is not uncommon to come across people who have a high degree of competence but little confidence; the opposite is less common. However, what employers need to ensure is a combination of confidence and competence.

The confusion between confidence and competence and between belief and expectation arises from the assumption that capability and ability are synonymous. Not so! Capability is a given. Ability refers to the learning of knowledge and skills, and the range and nature of knowledge and skills acquired are determined by the culture you are a member of, and by motivation, expectations and level of confidence.

Expectations can be realistic, unrealistic, absent or low. Realistic expectations centre on a person's present level of knowledge and set the next learning challenge just a little beyond that level. For example, a child may be able to put shoes on her feet but may not yet have identified the right from the left. The next step would be to get her to notice that each shoe is different. Unrealistic expectations are typically performance driven, with the emphasis on getting things right. There is a failure to appreciate that there is an achievement in every learning effort and that what counts most of all is that an effort to learn has been made. Unrealistic expectations make learning extremely threatening because the possibility of getting it right may be remote. In some homes and workplaces people's love of learning may be gradually extinguished by parents or managers having no expectations and giving little or no recognition to efforts to learn. Furthermore, because the parents or managers do not have expectations for themselves, the children or workers involved wisely assess that it is not safe to rise above their poor level of functioning. What is more common is the situation where parents and employers have low expectations and do not realistically challenge the children or workers involved.

Whilst the nature of learning and work expectations is a powerful determinant of whether or not people will retain their natural drive to learn, an equally powerful influence is how parents or employers react when children or workers fall short of, rise above or meet expectations.

Certainly, realistic expectations go a long way to maintaining people's love of learning and working, but this can be undermined if critical reactions follow failure to measure up to these reasonable demands. These critical responses can take two forms:

enmeshment of the falling short with the child's or the worker's person, and direct criticism of the failure experience. The latter is certainly the lesser of the two evils but, nonetheless, it poses a threat to future learning efforts and may result in the person cleverly devising protective strategies to offset that threat. Typical strategies are avoidance (with no effort there can be no failure; and with no failure there can be no rejection), compensation (with great effort there can be no failure; and with no failure there can be no humiliation) and rebelliousness (by getting somebody else to take on the challenge there can be no failure and therefore no rejection). Rebelliousness may accompany either avoidance or compensation. Another ingenious protective response is to become hypersensitive to criticism, act fearful and show visible upset when it is present. The aim of this strategy is similar to rebelliousness — get those who are threatening to back off with their critical attitudes.

The enmeshment of failure with person can be devastating to a person's eagerness to learn. Examples of this kind of reaction are 'Are you stupid or what?', 'Don't you see what you are doing wrong?' (said with exasperation), 'You're not paying attention' (said angrily). It is important to note that the non-verbal messages that accompany the verbal critical message lend considerable weight to the impact of the punishing feedback. Victims conclude from this kind of feedback that 'I'm stupid', 'I'm unlovable', 'I'm slow.' These self-labels often follow them for the rest of their lives and determine their inability to thrive occupationally. Someone who experiences enmeshment of person with failure may take up one of the protective strategies of avoidance, compensation, rebelliousness or timidity. Because the threats posed are great, the strategies may be employed to extremes so that avoidance becomes apathy, compensation becomes perfectionism, rebelliousness becomes huge aggression and timidity becomes utter helplessness.

Unrealistic expectations in themselves pose an enormous threat to the pursuance of learning and work, but when they are accompanied by punishing responses to failure to attain these high levels, the threat is greatly increased. Generally speaking, where there are unrealistic learning or work expectations, there is also the tendency to confuse person with failure. Criticism can be expressed harshly or great hurt and disappointment can be visibly shown. Powerful protective reactions are needed in response to these blows.

Positive over-reaction when individuals meet either realistic or unrealistic expectations is also a block to the emergence of confidence, but is often not seen as such. Examples are 'You're an amazing worker'; 'You're a cut above the rest'; 'You're great'; 'We're so proud of you.' The difficulty with these responses is that those at the receiving end of such accolades become dependent on their accomplishments in order to be deemed worthy. They also know that falling short would result in emotional rejection ('You've let us down', 'You're not a company man', 'You're a disappointment').

The possession of your power as an adult lies with your own affirmation of your vast intellectual potential and freeing yourself of those who, because of their own shadows, have attempted to block your capability. This is not so easily done, as there are many who may be frightened of you should you become powerful and who will accordingly find protective ways to hinder your progress.

CHAPTER 3

WHEN WORK DETERMINES WORTH

WORK ADDICTION

There are many kinds of addiction, the most documented of which is probably alcohol. The pity is that this addiction has become medicalised and therefore everyone is let off the hook in terms of responsibility for its causes and effects. It is surprising that other addictions — drugs, smoking, food, sex, gambling — have not yet been medicalised, but this is largely due to the recognition that these addictive responses arise from unresolved conflicts within and outside the afflicted individuals. The most unrecognised addiction is that to work, but, like addiction to alcohol, its effects can be devastating on personal, interpersonal and family development. The addiction to work is very powerful and it is difficult to overcome, because, unlike other addictions, those who are work addicted are reinforced strongly for their over-dedication. Work addiction can gain you phenomenal material and career success, status, praise and adulation. Where there is work addiction self-worth and work are strongly inter-twined and any conflict at work can pose a serious threat to emotional and physical well-being. For example, work addiction is associated strongly with heart disease in men and ME (fatigue syndrome) in women. The implication inherent in work addiction is that 'without work I am valueless and worthless'. Work addiction varies along a continuum of mild to severe, depending on how intensely the person approaches work and the duration of working hours each week. The main indicators of work addiction are listed below.

INDICATORS OF WORK ADDICTION

- ☐ Cannot say 'no' to job demands
- ☐ Works between 60 and 80 hours weekly
- ☐ Rarely takes a holiday
- ☐ Has difficulty in delegating work
- ☐ Takes work home
- ☐ Works weekends
- ☐ Is preoccupied with job matters
- ☐ Job dominates social conversations
- ☐ Misses meals due to job commitments
- ☐ Breaks off holidays because of job demands
- ☐ Is always available for job
- ☐ Is easily contactable by phone
- ☐ Misses important marital and family events because of job demands
- ☐ Shows perfectionism
- ☐ Cannot tolerate criticism
- ☐ Dreads failure
- ☐ Has unrealistic expectations of self
- ☐ Thrives on success

If you answered 'yes' to more than three of the indicators of work addiction then you need to seriously examine your dependence on work as a measure of your worth. The profile of the person addicted to work shows clearly that work dominates life and that all else — family, marriage, self — come second. The perfectionism, dread of failure, unrealistic expectations of self and intolerance of criticism mirror the underlying reasons for the addiction:

conditional loving in childhood and a sense of self that is measured by work performance.

I recall a thirty-year-old man who came to me suffering from high blood pressure, headaches and back pain which medication was not managing to control. He worked in high finance where pressures to perform are high. However, the major source of his psychosomatic complaints was his need to be better than anyone else in his field of work. He worked up to ten or eleven o'clock each night, including weekends. He was unmarried and was not involved in any relationship. He missed meals, ate unhealthily and had restless sleep. His mind was constantly occupied with his work. His father was a very successful self-made man and had demanded the same successful performance from his son from early childhood. His mother, a teacher, was a perfectionist who had unrealistic academic expectations of him. He had managed for years to live up to their expectations but at the time of therapy the costs were beginning to emerge more clearly: health problems, social isolation and personal insecurity. It took considerable time for this man to let go of his dependence on work performance and the even deeper dependence on his parents for his sense of self. Even at thirty years of age he was still the small boy wanting so much to please his parents.

The effects of work addiction can be physical, behavioural, emotional and social. The deeper the level of addiction, the more serious, intense and enduring these costs will be and the greater the risks to the person's overall well-being.

EFFECTS OF WORK ADDICTION

Physical
☐   Vague aches and pains
☐   Indigestion

➔

- ☐ Chest pains
- ☐ Headaches
- ☐ Stomach problems
- ☐ Back pain
- ☐ Shoulder and arm pain
- ☐ Arthritis
- ☐ Fatigue syndrome
- ☐ Multiple sclerosis
- ☐ Motor-neurone disease
- ☐ High blood pressure
- ☐ Heart disease
- ☐ Migraine

Emotional

- ☐ Anxious
- ☐ Irritable
- ☐ Easily threatened
- ☐ Over-wrought
- ☐ Hassled
- ☐ Jealous
- ☐ Fearful

Social

- ☐ Marital or relationship difficulties
- ☐ Little contact with children
- ☐ Few social outings
- ☐ Low libido
- ☐ Non-assertive or aggressive behaviours
- ☐ Few friends
- ☐ Difficult staff relationships
- ☐ Over-pleasing of or hostility towards management and work peers

---

Behavioural

☐ Rushes and races
☐ Shows aggressive or passive (sometimes both) behaviours
☐ Compensatory actions
☐ Sleeplessness
☐ Tension
☐ Always on the go
☐ Difficulty in relaxing
☐ Competitive
☐ Skips or rushes meals
☐ Works long hours

Probably the saddest aspect of work addiction is the absence of deep and loving relationships: work addiction is an emotional and social desert that must subconsciously strike at the very heart of the being of those addicted. However, if you are work addicted and you give priority to relationships, you risk the only acceptance and visibility you have known — the conditional acceptance received for work performance. It is clever to maintain that lifeline until you have established the stronger and healthier lifelines of unconditional acceptance of self, independence of the approval of others and separation of work from your worth. Conformity to the immature expectations of parents or bosses (who may represent your parents) is a protective force and not a weakness. When you achieve self-regard and independence the protective walls of work performance and approval seeking will automatically disintegrate. Paradoxically, when you achieve this state of equilibrium you will become far more successful, but without the costs to self or others. Happiness lies not in having your portrait hanging in the halls of the company that employs you or in material wealth, but in having the riches of loving relationships with self and others, and in the seeking out and the enjoyment of a range of challenges including work. Employers

and managers would do well to realise that creativity and productivity abound when performance anxiety is extinguished.

There is a major difference between people who love and enjoy
work and those addicted to it: the latter are driven by fear and the
former by challenge. Also, those who are motivated by the
challenge of work tend to have a balanced lifestyle. The fears that
drive those addicted to work are fears of failure, criticism and
rejection. They have been reared with the conviction that their
worth and lovability rest on how hard they work and how
productive they are. They tend to be performance driven and any
mistake or 'falling short' of targets will produce shock waves. Not
only will they not tolerate failure for themselves but they will be
highly critical of other workers' shortcomings. One of the
problems with employers who are work addicted is that their
dependence on work as a measure of their worth seriously limits
their creativity and entrepreneurship. There are no greater blocks
to creativity and productivity than fears of failure or rejection and
dependence on success. They drive people into being over-
cautious, rigid and inflexible. Those addicted to work will thrive
on tasks that are clear-cut but will be threatened by change and
uncertainty.

WHEN THREATS OCCUR

Over-work, perfectionism and performance anxiety are the main
hallmarks of work addiction. When any threat to work performance arises the person will react either passively or aggressively.
Threats within the workplace can come in the shape of deadlines,
change in management, new work structures, failure, drop in
performance, work appraisals, criticism, comparison with a
colleague, pile up of work or a formal performance presentation
to superiors. Threats can also arise from outside work: spouse or

partner complaining about work hours, children presenting with behavioural and emotional problems. If your tendency is to react passively to such threats you will shoulder all the blame yourself and work even harder to please your employer, spouse or children. You certainly will not voice inability or difficulty in coping and you will not assert your need for help and support. Passivity is an ingenious method of 'not rocking the boat' of your present ways of coping. Should you assert 'I need extra help' or ask 'What is it that you really need of me in this relationship?' the danger is that the protective cover of your over-working will be under threat and that the greater threat of rejection due to poor work performance will ensue. The latter would be too much to cope with, and so you bend your back to take on even more responsibilities.

The alternative to passivity in the face of threats to work addiction is aggression. Like passivity, aggression is a means of controlling others into not making more demands on you, but whereas passivity results in you taking on the blame, aggression projects the blame on to the other person. If your tendency is to react aggressively, then when pressures become unbearable either at work or at home you will complain hostilely about the other person's unreasonableness, selfishness, rigidity, stupidity and unrealistic expectations. The hostile responses are intended to get the other person to withdraw and to reduce their expectations. This is an extremely clever attempt to eliminate threats to not performing to par; there is no intention to hurt the other person but only to protect yourself from hurt. Following the altercation, work rate will be increased so that possibilities of future criticism, particularly at work, will be reduced. On the home front, aggression or a 'don't cross me' attitude will continue to be expressed in order to maintain the work addiction.

In less reactive moments, where neither passivity nor aggression is operating, confrontation on over-working may be met with ingenious rationalisations:

- □ 'We need the money.'
- □ 'Things will not be as difficult next year.'
- □ 'I really don't work that hard.'
- □ 'You only imagine that I'm not home evenings.'
- □ 'The company is depending on me.'
- □ 'The present situation is only a stepping stone to a less pressurised position.'

Rationalisations are wonderful means of diluting the seriousness of the situation and painting a far rosier picture than is the case in reality. The hope is that the person these are addressed to will take them on board and stop undermining the addict's dependence on work.

BURNOUT AND WORK ADDICTION

The tail-end of addiction to work is burnout. Burnout results when workers roll up their sleeves and attempt to cope with multiple internal and external demands. The main signs of burnout are listed below. In checking through this list it is important to evaluate the frequency, intensity and duration of these symptoms.

SIGNS OF BURNOUT

- □ Absenteeism
- □ Physical exhaustion
- □ Appetite problems (under-eating or over-eating)
- □ Insomnia
- □ Psychosomatic complaints (for example headaches, back pain, chest pain, stomach problems, bowel problems)

→

- [] Irritability
- [] Reliance on drugs such as alcohol, tranquillisers, anti-depressants, nicotine
- [] Pessimism and fatalism
- [] Increasing discouragement
- [] Defensive attitudes to work
- [] Poor relationships with colleagues
- [] Loss of self-esteem
- [] Loss of motivation to develop oneself
- [] Reduced involvement in life
- [] Loss of creativity

Burnout results from the combination of the enmeshment of self with work and work pressures. The help that is needed is the separation of one's sense of self from work and the development of a balanced approach to work. A supportive and person- and family-friendly workplace would greatly benefit this process.

CAUSES OF WORK ADDICTION

The *remote causes* of work addiction lie in the family of origin:

- [] One or both parents who were addicted to work
- [] Unrealistic expectations
- [] 'Success' important to family image
- [] Punishment of failure
- [] Over-rewarding of success
- [] Sibling rivalry
- [] Competitiveness

Identification with a parent who proves self through work is an ingenious way for a child to gain favour with that parent. The problem is that the child begins to believe that her worth lies in her dedication to work and any shirking will be viewed dimly by the parent who is work addicted.

Many parents live their lives through their children: 'My child will have everything that I didn't have as a child' (whether she likes it or not!). Such parents can put immense pressure on children to achieve highly in a particular area of knowledge — academic, sports, music, art, literature, professional acting. Examples abound of young professionals who burn out or become seriously psychologically disturbed or physically ill because of the pressure to succeed from parents. These parents have not let go of their adult offspring and continue to exert an undue and threatening influence on them.

A related pressure to the forgoing is the importance of the family image of wealth and success and the demand that children buy into that image. I recall a young man who dropped out of college and came for help in a highly confused and distressed state. There were six siblings in the family and all, except himself, had followed the profession of their parents. He had rebelled against this demand and had studied for an Arts degree. Nobody supported him; indeed he was seen as letting the family down. Furthermore, his grandfather, who was a well-known figure, refused to talk to him following his decision. The young man was ostracised and the isolation led to depression and apathy.

The strongest protection against experiencing failure is to try to be successful. Fear of failure has led to many people being work addicted. Such compensatory behaviour arises in response to harsh treatment of mistakes by parents or teachers. Harsh re-action to mistakes leads to the devastating experience of not being loved for self and creates the pressure to gain approval through perfectionism.

When there is much ado about success in homes and schools, children accurately assess that recognition is best achieved by being successful. When there is accompanying disappointment or ridicule in times of failure, then it becomes even more expedient for the child to please parents and teachers through high performance.

Sibling rivalry can be a driving force to be successful, particularly in situations where the way to please parents is through success. Comparisons between children by parents or teachers can lead to children seeking to outdo each other in order to be the one who is most cherished. Deep down, these children know that survival depends on gaining recognition by being 'one up' on the other siblings. Such savage competitiveness can also be seen in workplaces, sportsfields and academic circles.

The *immediate triggers* to work addiction may be the culture of the workplace, management style or sheer monetary need. Birds of a feather flock together, and it is often the case that those who are already driven by work performance are attracted to work organisations that reward productivity and place little value on the person. The combination of the inner and outer forces to be successful becomes a potent addictive potion.

A management style that is aggressive and driving in nature, and models and expects addictive work responses, makes it highly unsafe to have either a balanced or an avoidant approach to work. It certainly is too threatening to fail, and achievement of targets only increases subsequent expectations. Success here is a bottomless pit that is impossible to fill.

Poverty and marginalisation can lead people to have an over-emphasis on success and a need to please. This is often seen, for example, among emigrant workers. The consequences are severe when these workers do not measure up, and can include an even more meagre existence and economic and social dependence.

PROJECTION: A BLOCK TO PROGRESS

Work is a precious aspect of your life and what you work at needs to be worthy of you, deserving of your knowledge, skills, energy and most of all your dignity, and always respectful of yourself. When work does not meet these criteria you need to review your situation. However, if in spite of knowing about these boundaries necessary for a healthy work life, you persist in your acceptance of neglect, there are personal and/or organisational reasons for this persistence. The personal blocks may be subconscious or conscious.

You may read this book and apply not one word of it to yourself while at the same time see very clearly how much it would benefit others. This is an extremely clever subconscious strategy of placing all the responsibility for change on to the shoulders of others, so that you remove from yourself all responsibility for risk-taking. Indeed you may be vehement, judgmental and forceful in your assertion that all the problems in your life have got to do with the rigidity, selfishness, poor managing and indifference of colleagues, managers and employers. The fact that this block is subconscious makes it unlikely that you will see the reality of your own vulnerability, unless some crisis occurs that catapults you into having to find help. This reminds me of a man in his late forties who had effectively been demoted in his job and came for help because he had become deeply depressed. He felt he had dedicated his life to his work (which he had) and that his employer was to blame for his current unhappy state. It took him some time to accept that his own dependence on work had led to him becoming over-cautious and non-adventurous and that he was moved sideways because the organisation required a more dynamic person in the role. When he eventually became present to his unique self and free from having to prove himself through work, he returned to work with a new-found dignity and passion.

When projection is present it indicates a deep vulnerability around worth and work, and considerable sensitivity and non-judgment are required to aid you to belong to yourself. What maintains your projective behaviours are criticism and judgment by others: 'You're always complaining'; 'Nothing is ever right for you'; 'We're sick and tired of listening to you.' The more others attack or passively accept your protective behaviour, the more it increases. For change to occur, threats need to be eliminated and there needs to be present genuine concern and unconditional regard. Such a relationship offers you the opportunity to journey inwards and become connected to that deep, unique source within yourself. When that connection occurs, effectively when you belong to self, you will then not become in any way trauma-tised when your outside attachment to work or people is changed, qualified or taken away. You will be able to stand strong on the ground of your own interiority.

Letting go of projection starts with owning your work difficulties and seeing that change effectively starts and ends with self. It certainly helps, and in the case of projection is essential, that support and love are present to help you take on these responsi-bilities. Nevertheless, only you can do the journeying inwards. The more you seek out supportive people and structures, the more quickly you will discover your inner worth. Possible supportive people are a clinical psychologist, psychoanalyst, psychotherapist, good friend, valued colleague and loving life partner; possible supportive structures are a personal development group, assertiveness group, support system at work, informal group of workers who want change and a trade union. Establishing interiority involves an intense, enduring, caring, sensitive, valuing and loving relationship with self (see chapter 7).

CHAPTER 4

WHEN WORK THREATENS WORTH

AVOIDANCE OF WORK

When work threatens your worth it means that your early experiences of learning were traumatic and you needed to develop strategies to reduce the hurt, embarrassment and rejection. Avoidance of work is the most frequently employed protector and is far more common than addiction to work. Avoidance can be either indirect or direct. Indirect avoidance is where you act in a way that gets others to back off from making demands which pose a threat to your self-esteem. Direct avoidance is where you yourself act to minimise or eliminate risk-taking around work behaviours that threaten your well-being. Indirect avoidance is such a good tactic because you can always blame the other (supervisor, boss, colleague) for not letting you know what were their needs. Their reply that 'You are too difficult to approach' or 'It's like having to walk on egg shells to make a request of you' will be cleverly countered with 'That's your problem.'

Underlying avoidance is fear of work, because taking the risk to work means risking failure, falling short of expectations, not being good enough, others being better than you and not being loved. The fear of not being loved is the most powerful incentive of all not to work. There is amazing cleverness in avoidance strategies, because in not doing something you eliminate the possibility of failure and rejection. You might respond to this statement by asking 'Is a person not going to be disapproved of for not showing initiative?', but disapproval is far less of a threat than failure and rejection. Furthermore, once you begin to demonstrate endeavour, you have to maintain it, thereby increasing threats of humiliation and loss of love. It is wiser to remain hidden behind the barriers of avoidance than to risk revealing your real self.

AVOIDANCE STRATEGIES

Indirect avoidance strategies

□ Being argumentative

□ Exhibiting hostile facial expression

□ Showing timidity and fearfulness

□ Reacting shyly

□ Demonstrating nervousness and anxiety

□ Responding with verbal aggression

□ Becoming tearful

□ Showing extreme emotional upset

□ Withdrawing into hostile silence

□ Sulking

Direct avoidance strategies

□ Being late

□ Forgetting appointments

□ Sleeping out

□ Being careless

□ Voicing 'Don't expect too much of me.'

□ Being clumsy and awkward

□ Doing things slowly

□ Not volunteering to take on responsibilities

□ Demonstrating average or below average efficiency

□ Not being inventive

□ Ignoring colleagues' irresponsibilities

→

Indirect avoidance strategies	Direct avoidance strategies
□ Causing dissension among staff members	□ Turning a blind eye to wastage
□ Creating cliques	□ Developing an illness
□ Gossiping about manager or employer	
□ Sabotaging production	

It is important that employers understand that indirect strategies such as fear, timidity, shyness and pained facial expressions are just as powerful as aggression in getting people to back off from making demands that are threatening. The expression 'You can't even say boo to him without him being upset' bears out the power of these behaviours as less demands are made of workers who display such vulnerability.

It is not that those addicted to work do not fear work in the same way as those who avoid it. The difference is that those addicted to work combat the fear by eliminating the possibility of failure through over-work and perfectionism while those who avoid work reduce the possibility of failure by minimal or no risk-taking and reduction of people's expectations of them. In many ways there exists a polarised addiction process for those who are perfection istic and those who avoid. The former are addicted to proving themselves through work and the latter are addicted to avoiding work as a means of reducing rejection. Those who avoid find means other than work to be seen in this world, ways that are less threatening to self-esteem, such as sport, humour, hobbies, interests, conversation and music. Certainly, at a behavioural and attitudinal level those who are addicted and those who are threatened approach work in opposite ways. But at an emotional level both fear work and sense how much of a threat it poses to self-esteem. At this deeper, sometimes subconscious, level of self-esteem both are powerfully committed to not re-experiencing abandonment in the arena of work. Earlier devastating experiences in childhood underpin their extreme protective reactions.

Avoidance of work is not an all or nothing phenomenon. Depending on the depth and intensity of the fear of work, avoidance can vary along a continuum from minimal avoidance to average avoidance to total drop-out from commitment.

A young man in his late teens was referred to me suffering from a range of psychosomatic complaints and a total avoidance of work. He had remained at home for five years after leaving school prematurely. What precipitated the referral was that he had stopped going out of the house altogether and would not even go out to help his father on the farm. He gave no hand with chores about the house and spent his entire day watching television. The young man came to the session under considerable duress from his mother. Like his father, he was quite a social recluse. His father had no friends or interests or pursuits outside the home and the family did not invite people in. His father was addicted to his farm work and spent anything from twelve to fourteen hours daily, including weekends, at work. He was also quite a perfectionist, easily irritated and sharply critical when things were not done his way. It seemed to me that the boy's extreme work and social avoidance was cleverly designed to offset any failure or rejection in either area of functioning. Whereas his father was not emotionally present for his son, his mother erred on the side of being over-present and tended to over-protect and give in to her son's range of avoidant behaviours. She also did everything for him within the home. The combination of fear of his father's unrealistic standards and the subconscious demand by his mother that he be helpless and depend on her had caused this young man to develop the powerful protective mechanism of apathy. He just point blank refused to take on any work or social challenges. He did not even take his meals with the rest of the family and hid away on the rare occasion that a visitor called to the house. The young man reported having no energy, but this symptom was in keeping with avoidance: to experience energy might mean being precipitated into some action that threatened his self-esteem. Furthermore, it is true that energy rises to a challenge, and other than television this adolescent had nothing that inspired him.

Family therapy was employed in this situation because both the boy's parents needed to change their own patterns of work and their social and parental behaviours so that a safe emotional climate could be created for their son to begin to become adventurous. This process was slow as both parents were pro-tectively reluctant to see their need for change, and initially they attempted to hold to the premise that it was their son who had the problem and not them. I gently pointed out that they had always acted in good faith and that their shadowed ways were a legacy from their childhoods. Their son was presenting them and himself with a wonderful opportunity to be liberated from fears and insecurities.

It is not too difficult to detect when people are threatened by work. Ask them what they think about work, how they feel about it and how they behave around the challenge of work. Typical thought patterns for those who avoid work are:

- ☐ 'Work is a pain, a drag, a necessary evil.'
- ☐ 'I hate work.'
- ☐ 'I dread going into work today.'
- ☐ 'I wish I didn't have to work today.'
- ☐ 'Whoever invented work should be shot.'
- ☐ 'I live for the weekends.'

When I touch into workers' feelings about work I often hear about their fear, dread, helplessness, resentment, anger, rage. Some of the main behavioural indicators of work being a source of threat to self-worth are listed below.

BEHAVIOURAL INDICATORS OF WORK BEING A SOURCE OF THREAT TO SELF-WORTH

- ☐ Verbal expression of dislike of work
- ☐ Demonstration of little or no initiative
- ☐ Passivity at staff meetings
- ☐ Resistance to change
- ☐ Uncomfortableness in the presence of those in authority
- ☐ Minimal work output
- ☐ Average work rate
- ☐ Resentment when requested to do extra work
- ☐ Sullenness when criticised
- ☐ Absenteeism
- ☐ Poor time-keeping
- ☐ Preference for others to take lead
- ☐ Demands for considerable direction
- ☐ Adamant about own rights
- ☐ Clock-watching
- ☐ Theft

When workers for whom work is a source of threat look at how they feel about themselves in work, they may employ such labels as 'average', 'follower', 'not too bright', 'not ambitious', 'passive' or 'aggressive'; their employers may use the same labels.

Avoidance of work can lead to a flattening of your experience of life, a shadowed sense of self arising from the protection of having to keep people's expectations of you low to average, and a dilution of your vast power and intelligence. Some of the main effects of work avoidance are listed below.

EFFECTS OF WORK AVOIDANCE

- ☐ Shadowed sense of self
- ☐ Lack of confidence
- ☐ Loss of love of work
- ☐ Little or no ambition
- ☐ Restricted lifestyle
- ☐ Low to average earning power
- ☐ Resentment or cynicism towards those who are successful
- ☐ Disappointment to others (parents, partner, children)
- ☐ Low to average risk-taking
- ☐ Lack of motivation to inspire own children with love of work
- ☐ Psychosomatic symptoms (for example, frequent infections, migraines, constipation)

The effects of avoidance on your work performance, which cause serious losses for your employer, can include inefficiency, blinding yourself to the wasting of time and resources, unhelpful attitude towards clients, absenteeism and poor levels of responsibility.

WHEN FURTHER THREATS OCCUR AT WORK

One of the most threatening responses to a person's avoidance of work is to attempt directly to reduce or eliminate it. This may astound employers who can be at their wits' end because of losses due to avoidance. But it is crucial to see that avoidance of work is not the problem that requires to be solved. There are far deeper issues involved which relate to the experience of unsafety to be truly oneself in the worlds of work, family and community and the failure to be accepted for being real and non-conformist. It must be recognised that avoidance strategies at work are ingeniously created weapons which attempt to protect the person from job behaviours that threaten emotional, social, sexual, intellectual, physical, creative or spiritual well-being. This does not mean that colleagues have to agree with and accept everything a person says or does. But it does mean that while expressing their own viewpoints, these colleagues respect the other person's ways and do not seek to impose their own. At all times there must be no threat of rejection when differences arise. In the long run it will pay employers to find ways to help these workers to become secure in themselves and to restore a love of work and challenge (see chapters 8 and 9).

Many people experience dread when employers or managers express even realistic work expectations. Once the expectations are above the protective level of the employees' work rate, they feel threatened and will now have to invent new protectors or escalate old ones in order to remove the threat. Typical reactions would be to become aggressive or hostile, sulk, go sick or complain that they have too much to do already. These responses are designed to get employers to withdraw the increased expectations and to ensure they do not try that ploy again. There are employers who are nervous about asking certain employees to execute their appropriate responsibilities and these employers' protection is to put the pressure on the more passive and conscientious workers. Too often the latter, who will not protest, become over-burdened with responsibilities and those who avoid and are aggressive are 'let off the hook'. Yet another strategy is to carry out the requested responsibilities in such a haphazard and lackadaisical manner as to be certain not to be asked to do extra work again.

If even realistic expectations threaten those who employ avoidance strategies, then unrealistic ones are terrifyingly threatening. The greater the threat, the greater the protective weapon that will emerge. Outright rage, histrionics or prolonged sickness may follow unrealistic expectations. Sometimes the employee may seek a new job that will be less demanding. Employers can be certain that unrealistic expectations will not reap any benefits with these employees. On the contrary, financial and productivity losses are more likely to ensue.

Employees whose self-worth is threatened by work hate change and the introduction of any new work systems will evoke protective responses from them. Likewise, a change in management or the introduction of new staff members will be viewed as threatening.

RUSTOUT AND WORK AVOIDANCE

'Rustout' is the opposite to burnout but is equally devastating to the well-being of those who experience it. Its main characteristics are apathy and learned helplessness (a protective belief that as a worker one is powerless and totally the victim of a neglectful work organisation).

The main causes of rustout are remote rather than immediate, but there are work organisations that reinforce what happened in the past. Those who have 'rusted out' have lost the challenge and excitement of work and have poor relationships with colleagues, they put in a minimal amount of effort and see things as never changing. Like those who become burned out, they do not constructively confront, but they do regularly condemn employers who offer no creative alternatives. Some of the typical signs of rustout are listed below.

SIGNS OF RUSTOUT

☐　High job dissatisfaction
☐　Learned helplessness
☐　Apathy
☐　Hopelessness

➔

□   Frequent absenteeism
□   Non-caring attitude and sometimes cynical about work and
     work organisations
□   Avoidance of responsibilities and new challenges
□   Isolation from other members of staff
□   Non-involvement in or non attendance at staff meetings
□   Psychosomatic complaints (low energy, low blood pressure,
     poor appetite)
□   Reduced immune system
□   Depression
□   Highly protective self-esteem

Rustout is the tail-end of a stressful sequence and it would be wise of workers and organisations to be aware of earlier signs of stress and to take appropriate action or at least reduce the job stressors.

CAUSES OF WORK BEING A SOURCE OF THREAT

Work can be a source of threat to a person's emotional, social, intellectual, physical, sexual or creative life for reasons remote and immediate. It is important that both employee and employer attempt to isolate the reasons that lead to work avoidance so that appropriate corrective actions can be taken.

REMOTE CAUSES OF WORK AVOIDANCE

□   Parent who was work addicted
□   Parent who disliked or hated work
□   Harsh treatment of failure
□   Being labelled 'stupid', 'slow', 'no good', 'average'
□   Frequent comparison with 'brighter' sibling
□   Unrealistic expectations
□   Low expectations

➔

- ☐ Emphasis on performance rather than effort
- ☐ Much ado being made about success
- ☐ Physical beatings when work (for example homework) was not satisfactory
- ☐ Irritability and impatience around learning
- ☐ Subculture where employment was not considered important

Certainly, earlier childhood experiences mould present attitudes to work. Probably the most common causes of work being experienced as threatening are unrealistic expectations, punishment of failure, emphasis on success, and modelling by parents and other significant adults (grandparents, aunts, uncles, teachers) of either dependence on work as a means of gaining attention or hostility towards and avoidance of work. As already seen, children will either adapt to or rebel against threats to their being loved; either way, they get trapped behind protective walls of conformity or rebellion or avoidance.

It is not that parents and other adults should not have expectations of children around their domestic, school, social, intellectual, physical, emotional and creative responsibilities, but expectations need to be realistic. Unrealistic expectations are unconnected to the child's present level of functioning. Realistic expectations set the target a little beyond the present level of competence. Children see this as attainable and feel safe enough to take on the challenge. Unrealistic expectations set the target far beyond present levels of competence and demand perfect performance. There is no room left for mistakes and failure.

It is vital when setting expectations, and when supporting and encouraging children to meet them, that any error is regarded positively. There must be no criticism, scolding or punishment around failure. Failure may indicate that more effort and practice are required or that some adjustment in the learning is needed.

Maybe more patience is needed on the part of the child or the expectation was unrealistic or the child needed more guidance and support. Failure provides a wonderful opportunity to identify the blocks to progress. Once the focus is kept on effort to learn and this is encouraged, praised and rewarded, children will master any work challenge.

Whilst unrealistic expectations are highly threatening, low or no expectations can be equally blocking of children's progress. Low expectations are part and parcel of over-protective behaviour and, for survival purposes, the receiver learns either to conform to being helpless or to rebel and become pseudo-independent. The point about low expectations is that no belief is being shown in the child's vast capability; where belief exists it frees children to show their vast power to learn and work. Confidence is knowing we possess vast power, but it needs to be safe for us to demonstrate that power in the social systems in which we live. When it is threatening to be capable, we wisely act helpless or reject the system.

Low expectations can also arise from parents' own sense of inferiority. Because they do not risk having realistic expectations of themselves, they do not make demands on their children. Furthermore, it would be too risky for such parents to allow their children to go beyond their own level of development. This can be evident in employees, managers or supervisors who are threatened by anybody demonstrating more expertise, drive or inventiveness than themselves. To protect themselves, these people will not reward such progressive endeavours and will keep their expectations of workers low.

Apart from family influences, low expectations around work can also arise in subcultures where employment is not valued or in a poor economic climate where unemployment is high.

Dependence on success is rampant in our culture. It is not only children who experience profound disappointment, sadness and anger when success eludes them; the same reactions occur in adults. These reactions are readily observed in the academic and sports fields, but simpler challenges such as attending interviews, speaking in public or making new friends also reveal people's addiction to success. The pity is that so many opt out of challenges unless they are nearly guaranteed success. So many experiences are lost to people because of their dependence on success. It is the experience that counts; the outcome is a mile stone in the experience, but the road to progress in life is end-less. When success becomes more important than progress then everybody suffers.

Failure and success are integral and rotating aspects of learning and work. They must never be used as motivating forces since to do so has the disastrous effect of drying up love of learning and work and sending people into a spiral of avoidance or com-pensation or rebellion.

Actions always speak louder than words. When parents are addic-ted to or avoid or manifestly hate going to work, such behaviour is more than likely going to be imitated or diametrically opposed by their children. Whether children imitate or oppose their parents' patterns of behaviour depends on which offers the strongest defence against threats to acceptance. This is an important point. It is not always the case that people adhere to one defensive pattern (say, addiction). If, for example, perfectionism ceases to protect against failure, the person may switch to 'dropping out' or aggression. I worked with a man who had a highly successful career. Due to increasing work pressures he resorted to using illegal drug substances which affected his work performance and he lost his job. Later, when he had overcome his drug addiction, and in spite of his wealth of knowledge and skills, he refused for a long time to contemplate returning to work. He had changed his defensive tactic from perfectionism to total avoidance. Not surprisingly, his father, whom he had put on a pedestal, had been addicted to work.

A key point around learning is that the learner and others involved (parents, employers, teachers) must have patience and ensure that learning always has only positive associations. Absence of irritability, intolerance, impatience, dismissiveness, criticism, ridicule, cynicism, sarcasm, rudeness and aggression is imperative for learning to remain effective and challenging. It is the presence of praise, recognition, affirmation, understanding, patience, encouragement, support and respect that maintains a love of learning.

Generally speaking, the immediate causes of work being a source of threat reinforce the remote causes and in so doing foster further defensive reactions.

IMMEDIATE CAUSES OF WORK AVOIDANCE

- Authoritarian or *laissez-faire* management style
- Unclear communication
- Unrealistic or low expectations
- Success-driven work culture
- Nepotism
- Public humiliation
- Sexual, verbal or physical harassment
- Punishing income tax system
- Low salary
- Poor working conditions
- Poor staff morale
- Absence of praise and affirmation
- Punishment of failure

There are certain reasons why responsible working may not occur: low wages, poor working conditions, crippling tax system. But there are far more serious blocks to effective working and these principally arise, as in childhood, from the nature of relationships that are operating in the workplace. The kinds of issues involved are management style, quality of communication, level of respect for individuals, and nature of appraisal systems. Effective management approaches, effective communication, and work environments that are both person and family friendly will be dealt with in chapters 8 and 9. Suffice to say here that management that is not experienced as respectful, fair and positively firm deserves the reactions it gets — avoidance, rebellion, poor motivation and poor morale. Unfortunately, poor management also affects the individual worker, producing fear, insecurity, timidity and hatred of work — all of which seriously affect the worker's physical, emotional and social welfare.

Nepotism, whereby some workers are given more attention, perks and recognition than others, can trigger a whole range of defence reactions by those less favoured. Workers have remarkable antennae for detecting favouritism as their need is to be treated equally and fairly.

INTROJECTION: A BLOCK TO PROGRESS

As a survival mechanism introjection is the opposite of projection but is equally powerful in putting off the daunting challenge of change. Whereas projection protects by blaming everybody else, introjection guards by denigrating self: 'I'm useless and worthless'; 'The abuse I get at work is what I deserve'; 'I don't know why anybody puts up with me.' The subconscious defence in introjection is that you see yourself as so weak, so stupid and so ineffectual that you rule out any risk-taking. Typical reactions to a challenge are: 'I am the way I am'; 'It's beyond my control'; 'I'm too powerless to do anything.' Introjection is quite different from owning. When you own your work and work difficulties, you see things in perspective, you have a sense of your own power and you are realistically aware of the dangers of change. In introjection there is no conscious connection with your own dignity, intelligence and creativity, and to allow yourself to see the full reality of your situation would be far too threatening. Workers who introject tend to have an inferior view of self compared to the superiority complex of those who project.

Dissolving the protective force of introjection is similar to resolving projection: owning, accepting that all change is in your hands, and taking the actions needed to come home to the full presence of yourself. As with projection, the more interpersonal and system supports you acquire, the safer it is to take on the challenge of finding your own unique power and becoming independent of others and work.

CHAPTER 5

WHEN WORK IS SEPARATE FROM WORTH

LOVE OF WORK

Only when there is an absence of fear can a love of work be present. Fear entangles worth and work, and the more intense the fear the greater the enmeshment. Fear will be absent if in an individual's earlier experiences learning and work were rarely confused with worth as a person. In unconditional relationships there is no confusion between work and worth so that whether a work behaviour is being encouraged or discouraged, the attention is on the behaviour. For example, 'Yes I would like to see a greater effort being made with your homework.' This is done without any threat to the worth of the person learning or to the relationship between learner and tutor. When such non-threatening inter-actions around work and learning are maintained, then children's natural curiosity to learn and desire to work will blossom. When 'slips of the tongue' in terms of impatience with the learner inevitably occur, mature tutors apologise, reinstate the worthi-ness of the learner and heal the rift in the relationship.

Some people believe that promoting unconditional relating in the home, school and workplace is idealistic. However, this is not an issue that can be dismissed lightly, as the effects of conditionality are now well known. Certainly, adults (parents, teachers, employers, employees) are required to find the means and support to resolve their shadowed sense of self and to begin to work out powerfully from their real selves. When they achieve this, or at least are on the way to attaining such liberation, they will automatically begin to treat others unconditionally.

Is love of work a rare phenomenon? The answer is 'yes'. However, fear of work ranges on a continuum from low to great dread, and there are many people who have intermittent joyful experiences of work. Naturally, when threatening behaviours such as harassment, impatience or public embarrassment occur, then the light can quickly be extinguished.

The long-term effects of love of work are demonstrated by the 10 per cent of elderly people who cannot be distinguished intellectually, socially, sexually, productively or creatively from younger people. What distinguishes this group from their peers is a love of challenge and a strong sense of personal worth. Behaviourally and intellectually, this group continue to find new challenges for themselves throughout their long lives. They also possess exceptionally good physical and mental health. I recently came across a ninety-four-year-old woman who was studying for her third university degree. I have also come across a highly successful restauranteur in his mid-eighties who in his late sixties, two years following the death of his wife, remarried, moved to another country and started an entirely different career. When you look, such stories do abound. These elderly people, who maintain a progressive flow throughout their lives, never 'retired' from work. The age for work retirement is getting younger and younger. Nowadays a considerable number of people retire in their early to mid-fifties, even though longevity is increasing. A sizeable number of these retirees do not live long after their retirement. I believe the reasons lie in the absence of challenge. The human psyche needs a reason to live. This does not mean we have to work at a particular career for the rest of our days, but it does mean finding new challenges so that life continues to have meaning. These challenges can be physical, occupational, social, spiritual, intellectual, sexual, creative or emotional. The important thing is to maintain progress and excitement; the word 'retirement' has too much of a death-knell sound.

It is also unwise of society to assign people in their sixties to the 'scrap heap'. There is no rational basis for this and, eventually, any group that are discriminated against will rise up in protest and re-establish their rightful and meaningful place in society. This process is beginning to happen. I also believe that if the fall in the birth rate continues, the importance of the elderly to social progress will re-emerge.

People who love work stand out from those who are either addicted to or threatened by work. Their home, private, social, spiritual and work lives flow into one another in a dynamic and mutually enriching manner. These workers exhibit poise, sureness and balance.

INDICATORS OF LOVE OF WORK

- ☐ Is ambitious
- ☐ Is eager to learn
- ☐ Seeks new challenges
- ☐ Has high concentration
- ☐ Shows initiative
- ☐ Is highly responsible
- ☐ Is fair and honest
- ☐ Shows low absenteeism
- ☐ Is respectful
- ☐ Communicates directly and clearly

➔

- ☐ Is intolerant of injustice
- ☐ Is assertive about rights of self and others
- ☐ Has an enriching personal and interpersonal life apart from work
- ☐ Is conscious of employer's needs
- ☐ Is efficient and effective

You may think that the employee who exhibits these character-istics is 'God's gift' to an employer. This is not always the case, as an employer who is insecure and is protectively manipulative, controlling, aggressive, unfair or exploitative would be highly threatened by such a mature worker. The old adage of 'birds of a feather flock together' can be as true of the relationship between employers and employees as of other relationships.

There is an important distinction to be made between efficiency and effectiveness. There are some workers who can show meticulous efficiency in executing a task, but their over-conscientiousness and cautiousness can slow up effectiveness in production. A further point is that some workers can be efficient in carrying out a task, but miss out on a far more effective way of achieving their goals. People who love work are likely to be both efficient and effective.

The effects of love of work are wide-ranging and stand in marked contrast to those of addiction to or avoidance of work.

EFFECTS OF LOVE OF WORK

- ☐ Confidence
- ☐ Competence
- ☐ Good health
- ☐ Real sense of self
- ☐ Balanced and healthy lifestyle
- ☐ High earning power

→

☐   Progressive career
☐   Strong relationship with others
☐   Marriage and family life given priority
☐   Openness to change
☐   Inspiration of others to love work
☐   Resistance to conformity

A difference that can often exist between those addicted to work and those who love work lies in the area of confidence and competence. Those addicted can show high competence but they lack real confidence. They may give the impression of being confident but, when there is any dent to their competence, they can be thrown by the experience. Of course, there was no true confidence present, only a pseudo-confidence based on having to be always competent. Those who love work have real confidence because they believe in their vast capability, and no experience of failure weakens that conviction. Furthermore, failure is taken as an opportunity to improve competence, and this mature response ensures an ever-increasing growth in knowledge and skills.

What really stands out among those who love work is their good physical health, their rare absence from work due to illness or stress, and their balanced and healthy lifestyle. They not only love work but embrace all aspects of life, particularly the relationship with self and others. These people are also more likely to have more career changes. Those who fear or are addicted to work are threatened by change and are more likely to stick with what they know.

WHEN THREATS OCCUR AT WORK

Those who love work do not live in a fantasy world. They are well aware of the perils in the workplace that can jeopardise maintenance of their mature stance. However, in contrast to their insecure peers, they are determined and strong in upholding and vindicating their balanced attitude to work and life.

THREATS TO THOSE WHO LOVE WORK

- ☐ Being told they are selfish
- ☐ Demands to over-work or under-work
- ☐ Being labelled 'do-gooders'
- ☐ Disrespectful treatment of self or colleagues
- ☐ Bullying of self or colleagues
- ☐ Non-listening
- ☐ Being ostracised

A frequent protective reaction by others to maturity is 'It's all me, me, me.' This is quite inaccurate, as the person who has a balanced approach to life, while certainly being mindful of self, is equally and strongly mindful of others. Conversely, those who are threatened by work or addicted to it are highly concerned with protecting themselves from hurt and, consequently, are not in a secure place to be caring of others. The best ally you can have is a person who loves work and life.

A not uncommon threat is the demand to work late hours. It is not that those who love work are not flexible and will not respond to crisis times when extra commitment is required. But when the demands are continuous a firm 'no' will be voiced. This can annoy employers if they themselves lack maturity and, if they persist with their demands, they are likely to lose a rare employee.

A highly competent and conscientious mechanic once told me of demands by his supervisor and co-workers to not finish jobs too quickly and to stretch out break times. He resisted these deceitful practices and gradually found himself ostracised from the group. In another case, a young builder who was employed by a county council related to me that he was told to only half fill a bucket of cement and carry only one brick at a time. Both workers had been labelled as 'do-gooders'. It is very difficult to resist such a recalcitrant approach in a work culture. In both cases, the employees moved on to other jobs.

A notable strength of those who love work is intolerance of any behaviours that lessen an employee's sense of self or any attempt at exploitation. Any bullying, manipulation or passivity will be firmly confronted. When verbal action does not achieve equilibrium, physical action will follow (for example verbal or written complaint to higher management, report to trade union, refusal to work until the rights infringed have been reinstated, legal action). Whilst unions have been to the forefront in fighting for the rights of workers, their bias towards workers has often blinded them to the violated rights of employers. If justice is truly to be served then the rights of all concerned need to be considered. Certainly, ombudsmen and state labour relations bodies have tried to correct the unbalanced approach of unions. Of course, what is good for the goose must also be good for the gander, and employers' organisations need to be concerned with employees' as well as their own rights and needs.

Another notable aspect of those who wholeheartedly embrace work is that they will not ignore violations of the rights of others. In this way they can be quite a thorn in the side of employers who do not respect the person and rights of employees.

Violations of rights may be directly experienced, for example verbal or sexual harassment. However, rights are also violated when there is silence and passivity on the part of employers and employees on issues such as poor working conditions, low wages, long hours (with or without overtime pay), absenteeism and irresponsible work practices. It is still not widely recognised that passivity can be just as neglectful of workers' and employers' rights as aggressive behaviours. Examples of passive behaviours are non-listening, non-action on violations, timidity, conformity to unfair demands and turning a blind eye to problems. There is also a host of passive-aggressive behaviours which operate in workplaces and which are rarely tackled. Examples are gossip, slander, indirect bullying, marginalisation of co-workers, invisible sabotaging of productivity and rough handling of equipment.

It is difficult for mature workers to witness any of these inappropriate behaviours, and if their protests go unheeded, they will move on and find more healthy work environments. The loss is that of the workplace they have left behind.

CAUSES OF LOVE OF WORK

The experiences that lead to love of work are the opposite of those described for addiction to and avoidance of work. Conditionality is the hallmark of the latter and unconditionality the hallmark of the former. The causes of love of work can also be both remote and immediate.

REMOTE CAUSES OF LOVE OF WORK

□   Parents or teachers who demonstrated a love of work
□   Parents or teachers who balanced home and work life
□   Parents or teachers who challenged themselves in many aspects of life
□   Parents or teachers who related unconditionally to others
□   Parents or teachers who encouraged, supported and were positively firm on responsibilities inside and outside the home and school
□   Belief shown in the vast capability of human beings
□   Positive learning environments

➜

- ☐   An embracing of failure and success as equal and essential aspects of learning
- ☐   Emphasis on responsible effort
- ☐   A fair sharing of responsibilities within the home

The major influence on love of work is having been loved for self, but another powerful factor is learning to have confidence in one's vast capability. Belief in children's limitless intelligence is quite rare, and as a result most people lack intellectual confidence. This deficit has arisen from misguided notions of what constitutes intelligence. Intelligence has been defined in terms of verbal and non-verbal behaviours, with a major bias towards academic behaviours — literacy and numeracy. It is wrong to say that children who show high knowledge of languages and mathematics are more intelligent than those who demonstrate expertise in, for example, sport and mechanics. These are just different areas of knowledge. The tendency to see certain areas as stronger indicators of intelligence than others arises from the cultural bias towards academic attainment and subsequent success in the more highly regarded professions (for example medicine, law, science, physics) as measures of worth. Knowledge is not an index of intelligence. Intelligence is a vast capability. In the last fifty years, the amount of new knowledge areas that have emerged is phenomenal and there is no doubt that with the present acceleration in technology this will continue. The current notion of intelligence is that there are several different types — for example emotional, social, academic, musical, mechanical — but this continues to limit the notion of intelligence. It is more accurate to say that intelligence is a vast capability which has endless capacity to develop multiple areas of knowledge. Therefore, the person who possesses wide knowledge and skills in, for example, sports, carpentry and humour is no less intelligent than the person who is academically qualified. The confidence of children and workers could be boosted by affirming the vast intelligence of all and by appreciating the particular types of knowledge developed by each individual. Such affirming actions form the foundation for a fulfilling and challenging work life. When children's and adults' ways of individualising themselves are not seen or are criticised, then doors to their career development are being shut in their faces.

It is difficult to shake the confidence of workers who are balanced. They are often regarded by others as 'radical' but this labelling is a clever ploy by insecure people to distance themselves from what these mature workers say and do. An equally clever strategy of those who consider themselves 'superior' to others is to label those who do not agree with them as 'conservatives'. Use of this label enables insecure people to avoid listening to those who oppose them.

Employees who do not confuse their worth with work are often the 'movers' and the 'shakers' in the workplace and the ones who become the leaders. But often because of insurmountable odds in the workplace they move into self-employment or become entrepreneurs in their own right. Self-employed people live longer and are healthier than those who are employed by others. This is not surprising, as many workplaces are 'diseased' environments.

For those who are balanced and who remain employed by others there may be immediate causes of their equilibrium.

IMMEDIATE CAUSES OF LOVE OF WORK

- ☐ Good staff morale
- ☐ Regular and democratic staff meetings
- ☐ Affirmation by leaders
- ☐ Recognition of responsible endeavours

➜

- ☐   Just wage
- ☐   Valuing of personal and family commitments
- ☐   Flexible time
- ☐   Fairness
- ☐   Positive feedback
- ☐   Constructive criticism
- ☐   Direct and clear communication
- ☐   Opportunities for promotion
- ☐   Encouragement of initiative
- ☐   Bonus schemes

Such work environments do exist, and where they do even those who are threatened by or addicted to work may find themselves positively gaining from the organisation's mature practices. Those who are balanced will thrive.

CHAPTER 6

WHY PEOPLE WORK

WHY WORK?

Not only is it important for individuals to understand what motivates them to work (or not work), but it is equally necessary for employers and organisations to detect the whys and wherefores, advantages and disadvantages of the work patterns of employees. Such information can help both the individual and the organisation to capitalise on mature work patterns or resolve work patterns that are detrimental to both the person and the organisation. Not surprisingly, organisations are quick to pinpoint individuals who are low in motivation, fearful of change, difficult or aggressive, or those who exhibit high absenteeism or present with psychosomatic illnesses. But it is short-sighted of organisations not to detect also those addicted to work, as there is a high possibility that such workers will experience burnout. Organisations which fail to detect work addicts tend not to be family or person friendly and the work culture often strongly reinforces work addiction. Those addicted to work need to be wary because these kinds of organisations have no difficulty in getting rid of the worker who shows signs of burnout, regardless of the worker's age, number of dependants or prospects of alternative employment.

The reasons for working are unique to each person. Equally, each organisation has its own unique culture. It is important that both the individual and the organisation check out each other before embarking on an employer–employee relationship. Organisations tend to be better than potential employees at determining the 'fit' between the potential employee and the organisation. Generally, employees do not analyse why they work. The absence of such analysis means the hidden reasons for working may affect job satisfaction, productivity and staff morale. Similarly, employers who do not pursue such information are not in a position to offset the ill-effects when employees' reasons for working are immature or to capitalise on mature attitudes to work.

People may work for one or more of the following reasons:

- [ ] To prove self
- [ ] To belong
- [ ] To be different
- [ ] To be financially secure
- [ ] To be powerful
- [ ] To be challenged
- [ ] To be free
- [ ] To avoid intimacy
- [ ] To be average
- [ ] To fail
- [ ] To be difficult
- [ ] To want not to work
- [ ] To be balanced
- [ ] To be spiritual

Most people will tick off a number of these reasons for working. It is useful to order by rank the chosen factors on a continuum from 'strongest driving force' to 'weakest driving force'. The rank-ordered reasons that stand out for myself are:

- [ ] To be free
- [ ] To be different

☐   To be challenged
☐   To be balanced
☐   To be financially secure
☐   To prove myself

Earlier on in my career development my rank-ordered list would have been.

☐   To prove myself
☐   To be different
☐   To be free
☐   To be financially secure

Being balanced and being challenged were not motivating forces for me at that earlier time and, therefore, work addiction was high. I believe the source of my working to be free lies in having felt trapped as a child in my family and, subsequently, as a young adult in an enclosed monastery. Furthermore, I was reared in a singular Catholic culture where there were powerful restraining forces on being your own person and having personal opinions. Conformity was the order of the day. I recall in mid-adolescence wanting to break away from the constrictions of family and later on in my mid-twenties wanting to free myself from the shackles of Catholicism. My working to be different was a means of being non-conformist and was an added reinforcement to the need to be free. I never was and never will be 'a company man'. I ultimately attained my freedom by establishing my own private clinical practice and consultancy service.

Certainly, in the earlier years of my career, the need to prove myself dominated, but as my independence of people's opinions of me grew, this need became less and less a driving force. Financial security remains an important but not overwhelming motivating force, which, I have no doubt, is linked to the primary need to be free. Because being balanced and loving challenge have become important issues, the level of work addiction has significantly reduced but there are still times when the tendency to over-work arises. Fortunately, my wife works primarily to be balanced and her lifestyle and attitude to work keep me awake to my own need for change.

WHY WORK-ADDICTED PEOPLE WORK

Individuals who are addicted to work may work for several of the following reasons:

- □ To prove self
- □ To belong
- □ To be different
- □ To be financially secure
- □ To be powerful
- □ To be free
- □ To avoid intimacy

The fact that the person may not be consciously aware of hidden reasons does not in any way lessen the power of work addiction. On the contrary, when those addicted become aware of what drives them to over-work, they are on the way to resolving the addiction. However, such information will not be presented to the conscious mind until either internal or external changes occur which remove or at least reduce the emotional and social threats that underpin the work addiction. This is why work cultures that affirm and value employees can create the fertile soil for their personal growth.

The person who uses work as a means of being visible in this world has learned the hard lesson that 'My worth lies in my work.' This is a common form of compensation for the privation of not being loved for self.

The different reasons for the addiction to work lie primarily in people's early experiences of work in the home, school, wider culture or subculture. Some employees will have a family of origin that was largely dominant in nature, and a certain percentage of these will choose the means of 'proving themselves' to offset criticism and rejection. The extremes they went to in childhood to prove themselves are likely to be repeated in the workplace. Employers and managers will be subconsciously seen as the authoritarian parent figures who posed such a threat to emotional security.

The 'to belong' motivation to work is often a product of either not having felt included in the family of origin or being a member of a symbiotic family. I have worked with men and women who when younger managed the feeling of not belonging to their family by finding inclusion in their peer group or sports club and later on in work. A symbiotic family is where all members move as one and must show no spark of individuality or independence. The family members tend to dress the same, talk the same and have the same attitudes. They very much stick together and exclude outsiders.

An ex-monk once asked me, 'Why is it that I find it very difficult to be on my own and have a recurring yearning to return to the monastery, even though I no longer believe in religion?' He had left the monastery several years before and had set up a very successful business. On tracing his biographical history, I found that his father had preached consistently that all that mattered in life was family and that without it you had nothing. As pointed out, individuality and independence are taboo in symbiotic families, and this man had replaced his family of origin with the monastic family. When he came for help he was 'married to his work' but was missing the more intense close living of monastic life.

It is not wise to 'belong' to a work system. When such people are made redundant or moved sideways in the organisation, or when the business fails or somebody is promoted above them, they can suffer greatly and feel let down, bereaved, lost and helpless. The core issue is that their own belonging to the work system masks the deeper fact that they have not learned to belong to self. When these people are connected with their unique and powerful source within, they will deal effectively with any loss of belonging in the workplace. They will certainly stand on their own feet and take decisions that are worthy of their dignity.

There are workers who bend over backwards 'to be different'. This reason for work addiction arises from their inherent difference not being seen and celebrated by parents and teachers. People who have to work to be different are a long distance from valuing their own natural difference. Nonetheless, getting recognition from being behaviourally and occupationally different from others is a clever compensating way of avoiding total invisibility.

There are workers who have had dire histories of parenting or physical neglect due to parents spending their earnings on alcohol or drug addictions. Not surprisingly, financial security can often become a compensatory addiction for these workers and can underlie their work addiction.

There are other workers who desperately seek power because they lack charge of themselves. They employ power to cover up their feelings of inferiority and vulnerability. They are severely threatened by the competence of others and they often exercise unfair control over fellow workers and attempt to reduce their fellow workers' autonomy and independence. These people aim for positions of leadership but they treat their charges as objects and are bent on exploitation. As managers they employ their immature power to bully, to criticise, to threaten, to compromise workers' dignity and to sack them. In situations like this the workplace is a hostile and dreaded place to face into daily.

Some workers when children rebelled against being dominated by the significant adults in their lives; as adults they can carry the drive 'to be free' into the workplace and strive hard to get to a position where nobody has authority over them. However, they are still dependent on how others perceive them and the challenge to be free to be themselves and independent of others needs to be taken on.

Being addicted to work so as 'to avoid intimacy' is not uncommon but tends to be more evident in males. Many men have difficulties with emotional intimacy, due to either being smothered by their mothers or identifying with fathers who did not demonstrate affection, warmth and tenderness. Work becomes a powerful means of protecting against being intimate or being pressurised to express love. A frequent complaint of spouses of these men is that 'He is more married to his work than he is to me.'

Advantages and disadvantages of work addiction

There are obvious gains for the organisation that employs people addicted to work:

- □ High level of commitment
- □ High level of competence
- □ Willingness to take on extra responsibilities
- □ Over-conscientiousness
- □ Honesty
- □ Little or no absenteeism

But what organisations often fail to recognise are the disadvantages of employing the addicted employee. In my clinical experience 'dedicated' is better spelt 'deadicated', as those addicted to work are highly likely to experience burnout and life-threatening illnesses. The unscrupulous organisation may benefit in the short term, but in the long run it would be better served by employing a person with a more balanced attitude to work.

The disadvantages of work addiction which employers often fail to recognise include:

□ The difficulty for other employees of working alongside those addicted to work
□ The bottomless pit of attempting to affirm those addicted
□ Inflexibility
□ Hypersensitivity to criticism
□ Resistance to change
□ Reluctance to seek help and support when needed
□ Inability to say 'no' to increasing demands
□ Ignoring symptoms of burnout
□ Unrealistic expectations of colleagues

You might believe that employees who never miss a day's work are like gold, but they create an unhealthy work culture that makes sickness and any occupational, emotional or social problem taboo. Perfectionists who are aggressive cannot admit to problems; rather, they blame others or the system for their difficulties, thereby creating a conflictual atmosphere.

A particular difficulty for employers who have work-addicted employees is that whilst these workers neurotically seek affirmation and recognition for their tremendous input, their need is never satisfied. Some of these workers dismiss the positive feedback received, leaving employers frustrated as to what is required. Until they resolve their own self-esteem issues, the internal vacuum of feeling loveless will not get filled. What is equally difficult with employees who are work addicted is to broach work problems. People addicted to work will personalise such confrontations. Those who are passive will sulk and withdraw, and those who are aggressive will attack and blame others. Both types will work even harder to ensure no further criticism. Many managers and employers tend to tip-toe around these employees, with the result that issues that need to be voiced and acted upon are left slide. Such protective behaviours do not serve the employer, manager, other employees, the work-addicted employee or, indeed, the families of all employees. Work organisations need to have structures in place so that such neglect is not perpetrated. To depend on an individual employer or employee to break the cycle is not wise, as their sense of self may be enmeshed with work, thereby making confrontation too threatening.

The most common work addictions are the ones arising from a need to prove self, a need to belong and a need to protect self from intimacy by always being busy. As seen, the drive to belong is a displacement on to the workplace of the need to belong to a family. These individuals did not feel wanted in their original families and they cleverly and frantically attempt to be included as a valued member of the work organisation. There are other people whose need to give and receive love was harshly rejected in their younger days and who use work as a powerful means of distancing themselves from emotional contact.

Addiction to work arising from a drive to be different in order to be visible in the world offers employers the advantage of boundless energy and creativity. But such a person is like the butterfly that flits from one blossom to another. The extra disadvantage, alongside those listed above, is that such an employee lacks focus and can cause frustration through the need to keep moving on to something new rather than building on what is present. The people who over-work in order to be free are the least addicted, as their ultimate aim is to free themselves of the ties that have bound them. It has been shown that the determination to be free is often a reaction to an over-critical and controlling childhood and the protective need to get to a place where they are their own boss. The disadvantage to employers who employ those driven to be free is that whilst their commitment to the organisation is high, their deeper commitment to themselves will mean they will eventually leave.

Clearly, the work patterns of those addicted serve the powerful purpose of reducing threats to being accepted for self. What is often not appreciated is that once a person is in a protective cycle of addictive behaviours, it is not possible to progress towards regard for self and separateness from and care for others. Only when emotional safety is present over a period of time is it likely that people addicted to work will emerge beyond their protective walls. This is their wisdom, and no forcing or criticism on the part of others will move them; indeed such invasive reactions by others will only lead to a strengthening of their armentarium.

WHY WORK-THREATENED PEOPLE WORK

Those threatened by work may work for one or more of several reasons:

- To be average
- To fail
- To be difficult
- Wanting not to work

People who feel threatened by work have learnt that perform-ance is more important than their person. Their reaction to this tragedy is to engage in resourceful avoidance patterns that reduce the risks of rejection around work. People who are threatened by work have a much higher level of absenteeism than those addicted to work. Break times will be exploited by those who avoid. Extra responsibilities are seen as a major threat by those who view work as too emotionally risky. 'Going for the average' is one of the subconscious means employed to reduce employers' expectations. Typically, employers load responsibilities on to people who prove themselves through work but are reluctant to request extra input and commitment from workers who go for the average. The sad reality is that many employees (and employers) do not seek promotion, do not show motivation, do not further their studies, are not inclined to seek alternative employment and, generally, stick with what they know. These people have been deeply violated around performance in their earlier experiences in homes and schools, and this tragedy is too often perpetuated in work environments. The presence of criticism, ridicule, cynicism, sarcasm, verbal harassment and public humiliation only serve to reinforce the protective responses of those who have come to dread work.

There are some workers who, because of early experiences of extreme withdrawal of love on foot of failure, develop a defensive reaction of failing so that others can no longer have any expectations of them and, consequently, no reason to reject them. Too many parents, teachers and employers underestimate the amazing power that people possess to offset hurt, and this power can begin to operate in the first two to three years of life. Employers can be nonplussed by an employee who has been shown countless times how to perform a certain activity but on each occasion somehow gets it wrong. As with those who prove themselves through work, those who dread it may respond either passively or aggressively when confronted on their unsatisfactory job performance or when asked to do something new. The rationale of passivity is 'If I don't react then I can't be hurt more' and the rationale of aggression is 'If I viciously react then I'll stop them from hurting me.' Those who engage in passivity may be easily upset, anxious, timid or fearful and those who react aggressively may be insensitive, hostile or bitter, or have 'a chip on their shoulder'.

Workers who are difficult can make work intolerable for fellow employees and the employer. Nothing is ever right for these workers. They complain constantly, gossip and blame others for their own difficult ways: 'You can't please anybody around here'; 'People are out to exploit you'; 'Don't expect anything from anybody.' The lives of these employees have been difficult for a long time and they are fighting fire with fire in an attempt to extinguish being humiliated and unloved.

In recent years Ireland has managed to reduce radically its unemployment rate and many jobs now remain vacant. There is a realisation that the country has hit on the hard core of those who protectively do not want to work. This phenomenon may have its origins in families or minority cultural groups where work was not a valued ambition or where great trauma occurred around work behaviour. But not all the sources of apathy lie in the past. For example, teaching has become the most stressful occupation and there are teachers who have 'dropped out' through stress and illness and who have no desire to return to the profession. There are others trapped by family and financial commitments who remain in the workplace but hate their work and consequently put the hours in, but not much more.

Advantages and disadvantages of work avoidance

From the employer's point of view, workers who are threatened by work can be controlled and manipulated and will often accept low rates of pay and poor working conditions. Even those who manifest hostility and are difficult will rarely act on their aggression and will continue to accept poor working conditions. These workers also tend to maintain long-term allegiance to the organisation (change is seen as a threat) and, from an employer's point of view, 'the devil you know is better than the one you don't know'. However, particularly for conscientious employers, the disadvantages far outweigh the gains:

- Lack of Initiative
- Low motivation
- Slip-shod performance
- Absenteeism
- Formation of cliques
- Dishonesty
- Resistance to change
- Tardiness
- Hostile or passive reactions to feedback

'Birds of a feather flock together' and those who are threatened by work tend to group together, thereby strengthening their avoidance disposition. They can also be strong on trade union solidarity, as this safeguards their jobs without them having to make any radical changes. Little change is likely until either personal or work culture development occurs.

WHY BALANCED PEOPLE WORK

Those who have a balanced approach to work toil for some of the same reasons as those addicted to or threatened by work:

- To be financially secure
- To be free
- To be challenged

The difference is in the way those who are balanced approach work. Work, relationships, self and the environment are treated with awe and respect, but rarely does work take precedence over self or others. These workers have enough flexibility to recognise that at certain times a greater work input may be required, but they will not unduly postpone a return to equilibrium.

People who are balanced in work have had early experiences of emotional security where person and relationships were not sacrificed on the fire of conditional regard. Work and learning efforts were encouraged and praised without any threat to the worth of their person. When violations did occur, reparation was quickly made in the forms of apology and appropriate corrective action (for example return of deprived privilege). The overall philosophy was one that accorded primacy to the uniqueness, intelligence, lovability, creativity and social presence of each person. Work, social and environmental responsibilities were seen as necessary and worthwhile endeavours and any attempt to slide out of such responsibilities was firmly and positively confronted.

Sadly, only about 5 to 10 per cent of people experience such mature upbringing. Not surprisingly, the presence of respectful and equal contact between people is not too often found in schools, communities and workplaces. This is a reality that none of us can choose to ignore. Without such forms of relating the fallout is great: individuals possessing a protective and limited sense of themselves, troubled relationships, marital and family breakdown, dysfunctional workplaces, and loss of productivity and creativity. The more all of us work towards seeing the sacredness of every human person and the need for unconditional relationships between people, the more we will release power.

Advantages of work balance

You might believe that any employer would welcome an employee who has a balanced attitude to work. Not so! There are many unscrupulous employers who would be deeply threatened by such an employee. The worker who is balanced will not tolerate unfair practices, verbal harassment, poor wages or unjust demands. Indeed, certain employers would see more disadvantages than advantages in having such an employee. However, for the just employer or organisation the gains of employing workers who have a balanced approach to work are considerable:

- Assertiveness
- Commitment
- Conscientiousness
- Creativity
- Equality
- Fairness
- Flexibility
- Healthy ambition
- High productivity
- Initiative
- Low absenteeism

Certainly, some employers might resent that for these people work does not take precedence over self, relationships and family, but an organisation that is neither person nor family friendly is unlikely to keep the balanced worker in its employ.

WHY SPIRITUAL PEOPLE WORK

With the fall-off in religious practice there has been a corresponding rise in spirituality. Regrettably, over time religions became political rather than spiritual bodies, and it was inevitable that sooner or later their true purpose would be seen and that people would look further afield to satisfy the heart's ache for a spiritual meaning to life. It is an age-old pursuit and one that is unlikely to be ever usurped by any religious, political or scientific developments.

Buddhism is fast becoming an alternative to western religions. Buddhism suggests that there are five practices that are conducive to happiness in this world:

☐ To possess virtuous, trustworthy and faithful friends
☐ To have spiritual aspirations
☐ To be skilled, efficient, energetic, earnest and learned in whatever work one does
☐ To conscientiously protect one's income and one's family's means of livelihood
☐ To be content and to live within one's means

People who work to be spiritual use their minds, hearts and hands to help self and others — no matter what they do for a living. Spiritual livelihood helps people to make a life, not just a living. For the most part those who are spiritual are doing the work they love and are passionately engaged in working. They want their work to be basically honest and helpful to self and others.

There is not a great difference between those who work to be balanced and those who work to be spiritual. The former group may not necessarily have spiritual aspirations, but more often than not when they reach a place of balance the need for a spiritual dimension emerges. Those who are truly spiritual will also have a balanced outlook on life. However, there are those who attempt to practise spiritual aspirations but who have not come to an inner place of peace in themselves. These people tend to be zealots and preachers; however, rather than preaching to others they need to look to the state of their own well-being. They can create quite a difficult atmosphere in the workplace. In contrast, people who work to be spiritual quietly follow their own beliefs, are accepting of others being different and are not threatened by opposition.

The advantages to employers of having employees who work to be spiritual are similar to those outlined above for those who work to be balanced.

CHAPTER 7

FINDING BALANCE

GROUNDWORK FOR FINDING BALANCE

Most of us struggle with finding balance. This is not surprising since we are reared on a diet of dependence-making, and that same process is reinforced in the workplace. However, when I consider my father's working life in the years after the Second World War, I know that now there are far more opportunities than there were in his day. Because of economic circumstances and major societal and religious constraints he was compelled to stick to a life of work that in no way gave him the opportunity to explore his many skills and potential to find balance. Regrettably at that time women were tied to kitchen and church, and the notion of career development for them was frowned upon. It was an age when not only did people have to lie in the marriage bed they had made for themselves but they also remained wedded to the one job for life. Nowadays, people are likely, and certainly have the opportunity, to have several careers. They also have more opportunities and support to achieve a balanced lifestyle. There are excellent career services available and there has been an unprecedented boom in counselling and psychotherapy services. Individuals, couples and families are availing of these services to either enhance relationships or, at least, sort out differences amicably. I am not suggesting that we all need to go for career and personal counselling but I am saying we no longer need to remain stuck in dead-end jobs, relationships or work-places. Seize anything that will enhance your own life and the lives of those who are dear to you.

What is entailed in finding balance? Many would suggest that awareness of how you regard self and work is the first step. I disagree. At an unconscious level you already know whether you are threatened by or addicted to work. Your actions of avoidance or perfectionism bear out this knowing. It is not awareness you need but support for change. It is very difficult to go alone against the tide of how you are expected to be. Support can come from the most unlikely places. I am always amazed when people tell me about how I have influenced their lives, even though there had been no direct contact between us; it may have been something I said at a public lecture or on radio or television, or something they read in a book of mine. However, it is not what I said that effected the change, but rather that what I said connected with their own inner voice and hidden beliefs, and that confirmation gave them the support to act on what had always been their own conviction.

Support for change can come from a partner, friend, self-development group, colleague or indeed employer. I recall during the days of being under siege in my post in a health board, how nursing colleagues provided considerable support for continuing my own personal and professional progress. Support also came from senior administrators, but it was done covertly. My own life partner has been immeasurably supportive in times of doubt and despair.

Support allows you to consciously look at aspects of your life that were holding back your progress. Without the presence of love, listening, interest and belief in you, you wisely keep your wisdom at a subconscious level.

Where there is serious addiction to or avoidance of work, professional support for change may be required. However, some crisis may have to occur before particularly fearful people will seek help. Until that point they are protectively deaf to the concerns of or challenges from others.

Support in itself does not alter your work circumstances but it is a *sine qua non* for the next step towards change, which is identifying the level of enmeshment between self and work and how that is manifested. Earlier chapters of this book are designed to enable you to determine how shadowed your real self may be and what types of protective responses you have developed to cope with fear of work. You also need to explore the remote and immediate causes of why your worth and work may be enmeshed. From this exploration, for example, you may find that you need to develop more mature relationships with parents or employers and change some of the attitudes to work that dominated your childhood years. It is your life, and here and now you have the chance to live it according to your own dreams and wishes. Your exploration may uncover your shadow self, a lack of confidence, addictive or avoidant responses to work, and an uninspiring and unhealthy work culture. The challenge is to allow your real self to emerge, to be in touch with your power beyond measure, and to achieve a balanced approach to work. It is no small challenge, but one for which you have all the capability needed.

WILL MY REAL SELF STAND UP?

Allowing myself to be myself entails creating an unconditional relationship with myself. Many people say to me that unconditional love is impossible, a pipe dream and an unfair expectation. This response is a marvellous protection against taking on the challenge of unconditional regard for self and others. It is not an easy task, and not a lot of people either dare to practise it themselves or encourage the practice of it in others. It is this lack of modelling by others and lack of support and encouragement to embrace the challenge that makes the risk so daunting. When you make the effort to be unconditionally accepting of self, you are likely to find yourself asking: will others regard me as 'selfish', 'egocentric', 'full of myself' or 'self-obsessed'? If these concerns arise for you, it is vital to stay separate and see that should such responses from others occur, they are reflective of the others' insecurity. Love of self is unselfish, considerate and sensitive to the needs of others. It is the lack of self-regard that brings about such protective and blocking behaviours as dependence, selfishness, possessiveness, control, aggression, passivity, passive-aggression and neglect of others.

The issue of unconditional valuing of self and others is something that neither employees nor employers can choose to ignore. The absence of it means that workers (whether employee or employer) bring their unresolved emotional baggage into the workplace, leading to the emergence of a threatening work culture. Acceptance of self means being independent of others and it also includes intolerance of any behaviours that belittle people and assertion of the right to respect and equality. Employers should know that self-confident employees are responsible, conscientious, fair and committed, but that they will also campaign for just wages, good working conditions and effective leadership. The most evident sign of self-valuing is being real and not needing to operate from a place of shadow. This is the person who follows the dictum 'To thine own self be true, and it must follow, as the night the day, thou canst not then be false to any man.' Difficult staff relationships are created when employees and employers hide their true selves and beliefs for fear of ridicule. For employees, there may be the extra serious consequence of loss of job. Whilst it is incumbent on each individual to develop a respect for self, it is also necessary that workplaces become safe places for all to reveal their true selves, rights, needs and grievances.

How do you develop a caring relationship with self? In the same way you create a close relationship with another. Such a relationship entails:

- Love
- Devotion
- Kindness
- Listening
- Understanding
- Encouragement
- Belief
- Challenge
- Support
- Nurturance
- Treats
- Sharing
- Acknowledgment of specialness
- Gentleness
- Fairness
- Equality
- Remembrance of special occasions
- Respect
- Acceptance
- Recognition of need for privacy

When any of these aspects of a loving relationship is missing or its opposite is present, then conflict ensues; shadows are cast on the light of the relationship and you place yourself in darkness. As an adult, all the power lies with you to be in a place of light. Only you can let in the love and regard of yourself and others. There are many people who are loved by others but do not internalise such regard. It is not that these people do not want to be loved; on the contrary, they are crying out for inclusion but they have come from homes, schools and workplaces where no such regard or great neglect was present and it now seems safer to keep others at bay, no matter how loving they may appear to be. When others remain patient in maintaining their regard for such a person, often the breakthrough does come and the person does breathe in the acceptance from others. Those who, in spite of enduring love, remain in shadow are in need of professional help. It is their responsibility to seek such assistance. Work organisations are also beginning to arrange confidential counselling for distressed employees.

Lifestyle is a key mirror of your relationship with self; your daily activities tell the tale of how well you care for self. The person who has high regard for self lives life according to desirables rather than the shoulds, should nots, have tos and ought tos we were all raised on. The desirables are time for: self, reflection, nurturance, partner, family, friendships, work, interests, hobbies, physical exercise, sleep, rest, treats, special occasions, holidays and spirituality. People with high self-regard take care not to rush, fret, criticise, push, pressurise, ridicule, over-work or worry unduly. If they find themselves behaving in any of these ways they take time out to reflect and correct the neglect. Of course, there will be times when mature individuals will rush and race and do extra work, but they never allow it to become a feature of daily living.

In the early days of establishing self-regard, time management — of your personal, social, emotional, sexual, sensual, occupational, recreational, physical and spiritual needs — is a valuable support. Daily, weekly and long-range time-management is recommended. Daily management is needed to ensure a balance between work, relationships (marital, family, friendships), leisure, rest, sleep and physical nurturance. Weekly charting could be concerned, for example, with interests, hobbies, spirituality, weekend plans and significant relationships. Long-range planning is required for holidays, special occasions and long-term projects (for example buying a home, development of a garden, further education, career development).

When you are in touch with and expressive of your real self, everybody gains. When you remain in the shadows of self-doubt, resentment, bitterness and dependence on or alienation from others, everybody loses out, including self. The fostering, affirming and encouragement of individuality is the foundation of healthy and productive homes, schools, communities and workplaces.

FINDING CONFIDENCE

Whilst work competence is a *sine qua non* of productivity, self-confidence is the cornerstone that determines not only the maximisation of your potential but also how well you apply your knowledge and skill. Employees who are confident love challenge and meaningful work, and they learn far more speedily than those who lack it. Sadly, lack of confidence is common and it results in potential or competence being hidden and talents being buried. When people lack confidence they are slow to admit to mistakes and are not inclined to ask for help, direction or guidance. They tend to hide their lack of confidence behind a veneer of either superiority or inferiority. Those who act in a superior way pretend to know it all and will often take on tasks that are far beyond their competence level. However, any failure arising from their efforts will be attributed to others or to unfair expectations or to unreasonable management! Accountability is not a behaviour that sits easily with a worker who acts in superior ways. Neither does accountability rest easily with those who subconsciously adopt inferiority to mask their lack of confidence; it could expose their vulnerability and consequently is strongly resisted. Acting in an inferior way (for example 'I'm no good with people', 'Figures and I just don't get on well together', 'I'm not the person for that job') is a clever means of ensuring that not too much is asked of them. This reduces the risk of failure and the possibility of their lack of confidence being revealed.

Some workers mask their lack of confidence by high levels of competence. However, if these high achievers encounter failure or criticism, they can react violently or show considerable hurt or major anxiety. Sometimes they go sick or may leave their jobs. These reactions reveal the pseudo nature of their confidence. Employees and employers who are truly confident respond to failure and constructive criticism as opportunities for further learning and skills development. When criticism is unjust or destructive, they assert their position and their rights to respect and direct, clear and fair communication.

Lack of self-confidence can be either specific to particular responsibilities (for example mathematical, social or leadership activities) or generalised so that nearly all responsibilities are seen as threatening.

Lack of confidence can be detected in such behaviours as:

- Fear of failure
- Fear of criticism
- Dependence on success
- Over-pleasing of employers
- Avoidance of challenges
- Difficulty in saying 'no'
- Over-working
- Anxiety when supervised
- Anxiety about deadlines or targets
- Under-achievement
- Blaming others for shortcomings
- Absenteeism at busy times
- Little ambition or over-ambition

It can be seen from this list that lack of confidence can be extremely crippling of both personal and career progress. From the work organisation's point of view, it results in multiple problems: poor productivity, stressed employees, poorly motivated staff, absenteeism and difficult staff relationships.

Clearly, confidence-building is a concern not only for the individual employee but also for the work organisation. Employees who are sure of themselves bring to the workplace maturity, high competence, ambition, responsibility, drive, enthusiasm, creativity, fairness, love of challenge and openness. Finding confidence is a matter of getting in touch with what has always been there – your vast intellectual and behavioural potential. Confidence has nothing to do with competence; it has got to do with accessing your limitless capability.

Labelling of individuals as 'fool', 'stupid', 'slow', 'weak', 'incompetent', 'useless' or 'dumb' is grossly damaging of confidence and totally inaccurate. It is true that individual workers may demonstrate a low knowledge or skills level, but they always have the endless capability to develop the competences required if given a chance and shown belief in them. These latter requirements are frequently lacking, and impatience and attitudes of 'You couldn't teach them anything' or 'You'd only be wasting your time' become self-fulfilling prophecies. Certainly, it can sometimes be the case that workers are slow to apply themselves or to develop required skills. The reasons for these responses do not lie in lack of potential but in their own poor sense of themselves and lack of confidence. Personal development and empowerment need to precede exposure to the acquisition of work skills.

The facilitation of self-confidence by employers and work organisations requires:

□   Frequent affirmation of employees' vast intellectual and behavioural potential

- ☐ Embracement of failure as an integral step in the development of competence
- ☐ Acceptance of success and failure as equally integral steps in the acquisition of skills
- ☐ Emphasis on and encouragement and praise of work efforts
- ☐ Recognition that confidence and competence are separate issues
- ☐ Acknowledgment of the influence that level of confidence has on productivity, career progress and job satisfaction

RESISTING CONFORMITY

The pressure to conform flattens people's individuality, creativity, productivity, confidence, drive, ambition and adventurousness. It makes puppets of people whereby they allow themselves to be pulled hither and thither, depriving them of any sense of being in charge of their own lives. Many work cultures demand total loyalty but such a policy is beneficial to neither the organisation nor the individual employee. Evidence in support of this is the fact that self-employed people live longer.

It is probably the case that workers who have come from home, school and community cultures that wanted sameness will choose similar work organisations. It is not just a case of 'the devil you know is better than the devil you don't know', but people who conform have learned the bitter lesson that being different is a punishing experience. Ironically, it is in being different that greater life and job satisfaction is achieved.

Resistance to conformity is one of the indicators of personal maturity. Such a posture must not be confused with rebelliousness or rigidity where workers will resist all or most demands for change. Mature workers will give fair consideration to new work demands, but they are not 'yes people' and their response will come from a place of choice rather than from the external pressure to conform. Work organisations would do well to promote such freedom, as self-motivated and self-directed workers are more responsible and productive than conformist workers.

Because most people are reared in emotional, social and work cultures that expect conformity, the first step in developing self-direction is to evaluate your present inclination to live your life according to the expectations of others. The more 'no' answers you give to the following list of questions the higher your need to conform:

- ☐ Do you say 'no' to unfair requests?
- ☐ Do you say 'no' to fair requests when other considerations are more important?
- ☐ Do you express your own needs, opinions or grievances?
- ☐ Do you demand a fair day's wage for a fair day's work?
- ☐ Do you consider other people as important as yourself?
- ☐ Do you value your own beliefs?
- ☐ Do you give fair consideration to the beliefs and demands of colleagues and employers?
- ☐ Do you reflect frequently on your life choices (including career)?
- ☐ In making decisions, do you go by your own intuition?
- ☐ Do you live your own life?
- ☐ Do you realise that shoulds, should nots, musts and ought tos are indicative of dependence and are ill-advised?

Resistance to conformity does not mean not caring for others. On the contrary, those people who are self-motivated are as considerate of others as they are of themselves; they wish also for others to possess the freedom to be and act themselves. Knowing you have the right to live your own life is not enough. Acting on that right is the real test, as you will face considerable opposition.

Recalling Nelson Mandela's words that 'your playing small does not serve this world' (nor yourself) may help you to stick to your task. Your own level of self-regard is the launch pad to non-conformity. Choice of friends, partner and work organisations that reinforce individuality, inventiveness, intuition and freedom to be true to self makes it easier to maintain your independence.

GIVING WORK ITS PROPER PLACE

The worker who is balanced is in a position to see that work is but one of a number of important aspects of living. Relationships, family, spirituality and healthy lifestyle are considered primary and are not jeopardised by work.

A typical week for a person with a balanced lifestyle would include the following:

- Maximum eight-hour working day
- Weekends free
- Adequate break-time for lunch (one hour)
- Daily time with partner
- Daily time with children
- Daily time with self
- Daily time for physical exercise (minimum 30–40 minutes)
- Contact with friends and family of origin (weekly/fortnightly)
- Two to three social outings weekly
- Healthy daily diet
- Eight hours' rest and sleep daily
- Adequate time for breakfast and commuting each morning

A schedule as balanced as this one is a rare occurrence. This is not surprising, as most of us are driven by insecurities and fears, and creating a healthy approach to work means risking a battery of hostile responses. It seems easier to give in and make the best of limited social and occupational circumstances.

Giving work its proper place demands a freeing of self from the shackles of work being either a measure of or a threat to your sense of worth. This is done by developing a respect and regard for self that is not determined by what you do but by your unique person and by seeking out relationship and social systems (work, community, educational, spiritual) that support that process. The reason why most people find it threatening to risk change is that it can be difficult to find such life-enhancing relationships and social systems. For this reason achieving a balanced lifestyle needs to be both an individual and a collective responsibility. The more work organisations enhance the individual presence of each worker and create a group presence that supports that process, the greater will be the level of job satisfaction and productivity.

STAYING SEPARATE

Separateness is the basis for maturity, for effective relationships and for a balanced attitude to work. Separateness means more than keeping your person and work apart. It includes not confusing another person's behaviour as being about you.

A young woman once came to me for help in a highly agitated state because no matter how much she achieved at work it was never enough for her employer. She felt useless, a failure, and had handed in her notice. The problem here was that the unrealistic and critical behaviour of her boss was being internalised by the young woman and hence her feelings of devastation. Her employer's behaviour was reminiscent of the young woman's mother whom she had never managed to please. In hearing her boss's comments as being about her inadequacies, she had become embroiled in the insecure worlds of her employer. Separateness would have aided this young woman to see that she is conscientious, creative and dynamic at work (which she is), and that her employer's unrealistic demands are a mirror of the employer's own dependence on performance for which the young woman is not responsible. What she needed to do was assert her position strongly, follow through in action and return solidly to her employer the ineffective management responses: 'I know there may be reasons why you are being unrealistic and critical but I know how well I have worked and I am not taking on board any of the things you have said. I will listen to realism and fairness and equality.' Tall order, you may say, and it is true that its implementation cannot occur unless the young woman feels good about and confident in herself.

The realisation that the words and actions of the other person are always about that person and not about you is a wonderful revelation. Not only does it help you avoid getting trapped into personalising what the other person is saying, but it makes it possible to keep open the door of communication. When you internalise a message from another person, you lose possession of yourself and communication breaks down immediately as you now either focus on how hurt you feel or attack back. When you know that what the other person is saying is about that person, you are in a strong position to try to get to the real message intended. For example, if your boss says 'Your level of commitment is poor', his message, though direct, is not at all clear. He is attempting to put all the responsibility on you and is not at all owning his own needs. In attempting to stay separate, the reply to his criticism could be: 'What makes you say that?' A possible retort would be: 'You are never around when I need something done quickly.' The original criticism has now changed somewhat but is still projective in nature. You could now seek further clarification: 'What are the things you need done quickly and how could we come to some definite arrangement that I am on hand to respond to your need?' This response puts the ball back in his court so that he now has to take responsibility for his need: 'Well, maybe immediately after lunch at 2 p.m. we could meet and I can let you know whether I have things that need to be done promptly.' By keeping communication open, through not internalising the criticism, you have managed to get to the real message hidden in the original criticism. Appropriate action can now be taken that will resolve the difficulty. If you respond to your employer's first message with a response such as 'You can't expect me to be in two places at the one time', this could lead to a counter-sarcastic response such as 'You're never where you're supposed to be.' Hurt now is escalating, neither of you feels heard by the other, and tempers may flare or you may walk off in a sulk. Because communication has broken down, nothing will be resolved.

Separateness is the basis for effective communication and is achieved by:

□   Realisation that a message (whether praising or critical) from another is not about you but about the person sending it.
□   Acknowledgment that a message (whether praising or critical) from you to another is about you and not the receiver.
□   Use of 'I' and direct and clear communication when sending a message.
□   Determination not to internalise what another says as being about you.
□   Genuine efforts to keep communication open.

You may ask: Is it always true that no matter what another says it is about that person and not about me? When, for example, my employer praises me — for instance 'I'm impressed by your level of skill' — surely the message is about me as the person who possesses the expertise? The point here is that, though you do indeed possess the praised expertise, it is a statement arising from your employer's perception. You can enjoy the fact that your boss sees your competence; or, as often happens, you may perceive your level of skill as being not as high as your employer believes it to be. Whose perception is now correct? The answer is both. It is important that you acknowledge your employer's compliment but your own assessment of your skill level may be truer for you. Employers who are balanced are both affirming of self and appraising of their own work efforts and skills, and they do not depend on or wait for their employer to recognise their worth and work. Nonetheless, it is a bonus when an employer acknowledges a worker's person and work. For workers who do not have strong regard for self and who do not appraise their own competence, affirmation and praise from employers, supervisors or colleagues may be the necessary platform to launch their journey of self-discovery.

PART III

WORK ORGANISATIONS AND WORTH

'All work is empty save when there is love,
for work is love made visible.'

Kahlil Gibran

CHAPTER 8

WORK CULTURES

THE NATURE OF WORK CULTURES

The family culture is the most powerful culture of all and its effects give light and shadow to the lives of its members to death's door. Other cultures that strongly influence people's lives are the school and the classroom. It is often the case that an individual teacher's classroom culture differs markedly from that of the school and has greater positive or detrimental effects on its members. Likewise, the community culture can operate to the benefit or the detriment of its members. Work cultures are no different. All cultures are complex and operate in times of turbulence and rapid economic, social, religious, political and technological change.

Work culture is both similar to and different from family, school, ethnic, national and religious cultures. It is similar in its foundation in values, traditions and basic assumptions, but it is different from other cultures in the sense that it focuses on work life rather than on every or most aspects of living. Nevertheless, workers come to the workplace not only with their work issues, but with their personal, family, school, community, ethnic, national and religious cultural baggage. This may cause clashes when the values of the other cultures of which workers are members are diametrically opposed to those of the work culture. Awareness of these potential value differences can help to anticipate, prevent or resolve conflicts for employers, managers and employees. Indeed, one of the recommendations I make to those going for job interviews is to make sure that the selection process is two-way and to enquire into the nature of the organisation's management and culture. Many employers express anger at the notion that they too need to be interviewed by potential employees, but the wise employer will quickly see the maturity of such an applicant.

Work cultures, like all cultures, are difficult to define. They are not easily discerned; what you see is not what it is all about. A work culture is made up of the symbols, language, assumptions, traditions and behaviours that overtly show the work culture's standards and values. It is a pattern of basic assumptions or behaviours that have been seen to work in the past and are taught to new entrants as the right way to perceive, to think, to feel and to act. When such cultures are not caring in nature they can have profound effects on the well-being of all members. Certainly, it is essential to check a work organisation's beliefs on:

☐ The nature of the person
☐ The nature of human relationships
☐ Style of management
☐ The relationships between the organisation and its members
☐ The relationship between the organisation and the community
☐ The couple relationship
☐ The family
☐ Balanced lifestyle
☐ Spirituality
☐ Vulnerability

For example, does the work culture regard people as unique, sacred and essentially good or does it see humans as basically weak and in need of control? Does it see its function as providing employment to a community or exploiting the community for its own profit-making, research and learning? Does the organisation see the unlimited potential of human beings or does it believe that people are not to be trusted and require an authoritarian management approach? Is the organisation person, family and relationship friendly or does it view profit as more important than people? And what is its attitude to employees who work to be balanced and spiritual or to those who are threatened by or have to prove themselves through work? These are examples of the many questions that potential employees could explore.

It is fascinating how work cultures have developed particular metaphors or symbols that amazingly compress complex issues into simple images. Common work culture metaphors are:

- Militaristic
- Athletic
- Social
- Mechanistic
- Animalistic

Work cultures characterised by a military metaphor refer to leaders as chiefs or captains of the ship and managers as lieutenants. Popular phrases used are 'It's a war out there', 'We run a tight ship here' or 'People have to tighten their belts in here'. Employees are viewed as the troops or foot soldiers. Motivating language extends the militaristic symbolism. 'It's tough in the trenches', 'Guard your rear end'. Managers and employees talk about battles won or campaigns lost and are on the lookout for sabotage. Rewards are given for 'bravery' or 'being ahead of the posse'.

In the workplace typified by a sports metaphor, the workforce is referred to as the team, and managers and supervisors as captains and coaches respectively. Teamwork, pulling your weight and task forces are especially valued. Although a few 'stars' are permitted to emerge from the team, being a good team player is regarded as being more important. This workplace values annual rallies, team-building exercises and award ceremonies at which workers are expected to show enthusiasm and which may be helped along by 'cheerleaders', whose task is to generate high morale and team spirit. Such companies may have team colours, banners and even a company song. Playing and winning the game is what it is all about and those who do not play well may be firmly sidelined. This work culture is akin to the symbiotic family where sameness is the rule, individuality is viewed as a major threat and any attempt to free yourself leads to total exclusion. Workers who are members of a symbiotic work culture often complain that the organisation demands total allegiance and is not considerate of the worker's personal, interpersonal and family lives.

The 'one big happy family' organisation is an example of a culture typified by a social metaphor. Newcomers are the kids, the top administrator is big daddy or big mamma, and favourite employees are family pets. There are also aunts and uncles who are there to aid workers to get what they need from big daddy who controls finances, or from big mamma who makes the rules. Elders know best but, like many parents, will only respond positively if employees follow the company's rules or take their counsel. Rewards are provided especially for supporting the integrity of the 'family', for long service and for loyalty. Organisational get-togethers, like Christmas parties, are integral to the culture. Employees who do not measure up to the 'family' expectations and who leave the company are not welcomed back at any time, whilst those who were loyal and leave are always welcome to return. Nepotism is common and those on the inside are nurtured for and promoted to top positions to the exclusion of those on the outside.

Mechanistic-type cultures are revealed by the use of metaphors such as 'This place is run like a well-oiled machine', 'You're just a spoke in the wheel here', 'It's just an assembly line' or 'Everything is done like clockwork here.' Rigid conformity to norms and values is expected.

A rarer type of organisation is the one characterised by animalistic metaphors. In this type, the organisation may be referred to as a zoo and members may include the top cat or top dog, the lion king, the work horse, busy bees, the chicken, the sacrificial lamb. Common phrases include 'They work us like dogs here', 'This place is like being trapped in a bird cage', 'An odd time they thrown us a bone' or 'When you fail, you get thrown to the wolves.' This type of company is largely unfeeling in nature and is akin to an emotionless family culture where the emphasis is on physical caring with no room for intimacy. Such a home or work culture is seriously neglectful of members' emotional and social welfare. This work organisation is an example of 'profits before people.'

Perhaps because there are not too many examples of person-centred work organisations, metaphorical representations of such a culture have not yet evolved. Whilst there is a growing recognition that work cultures need to broaden their perspective to include the personal and cultural baggage that workers, managers and employers bring to the workplace, the emphasis still tends to be on how to maximise productivity. Human resources management, personnel departments and sophisticated selection systems tend to be geared towards the needs of the organisation. These developments, albeit a step in the right direction, are appended to the organisation's culture, rather than being an integral part of it and a source of philosophical challenge.

WORK CULTURES AND WORKERS' WORTH

Each of the six types of work cultures identified has its own particular patterns of management and communication:

- □ *Militaristic*: dominant; controlling; vertical/downward communication
- □ *Athletic*: symbiotic demands; vertical/downward communication
- □ *Social/happy family*: over-protective; downward/upward communication
- □ *Mechanistic*: emotionally uncaring; emphasis on productivity and material rewarding
- □ *Animalistic*: abusive communication; neither emotionally nor physically caring; ruthless; focuses on productivity and exploitative communication
- □ *Person-centred*: egalitarian; democratic; open and direct communication

The militaristic and athletic-type cultures are conditional in nature; once you 'toe the line', your conformity will gain you conditional regard, respect, promotion and financial rewards. However, neither culture allows for personal independence, initiative and creativity. The advantages these work cultures offer to members are financial security, possibility of promotion and long-term employment in return for loyalty and conformity. The disadvantages are loss of independence, being valued not for self but for what you do, fear of not measuring up, dependence which makes it difficult to break away and a suppression of your personal uniqueness and vast power. There is some token recognition of personal, relationship and familial needs. The symbiotic organisation does provide comfort and can be fair in paying just wages, but sameness, extinction of individuality and total dedication to the organisation are demanded.

Individuals attracted to a dominant-controlling culture will tend to be those who work:

□   To prove themselves
□   To be financially secure
□   To be average
□   To be free

Those attracted to the family-type work culture will tend to be those who have a history of being cosseted and have a poor sense of competence and confidence. They come with one or more of the following needs:

□   To belong
□   To be financially secure
□   To fail
□   To not want to work

The emotionally uncaring but physically caring (mechanistic) and totally exploitative (animalistic) work cultures provide no nurturance, respect or valuing of human beings. Neither do they emotionally reward human endeavour. Verbal and physical harassment rule the workers and any attempt to confront injustice is dealt with viciously or harshly.

None of these cultures is person, relationship and family friendly.

RIGHTS THAT AFFIRM WORTH

Whilst it is the responsibility of each individual worker to invite and accept behaviours that affirm their worth and to strongly reject any response that undermines their person, it is also incumbent on the employer and work organisation to respect workers. This does not mean that employers lose sight of the primary focus of the organisation — maximum productivity — but this focus is maintained against a backdrop of respect for all within the work system. There also needs to be realistic recognition that workers have important personal, social and familial responsibilities outside of work, and accommodation must be made for important events, for example birth of a child, marriage or a crisis (for instance family member seriously ill or psychologically distressed or children unwell). Many employers and managers worry that creating an environment of care for workers means being 'soft'. There is the added problem that most employers and managers are males who are uncomfortable with emotional expressions of regard and who protectively use a 'tough' approach. Aggression, dominance, humiliating criticism, putting people down, verbal harassment or threatening behaviours are no longer acceptable forms of interaction, whether between employers and employees or between employees themselves. In any case, such behaviours are counter-productive; their effect is to breed resentment, bitterness, counter-aggression, anxiety, thoughts of revenge and sometimes sabotage. In America the most frequent cause of death in the workplace is murder. There is also an epidemic of work-related illnesses. It is time that employers and managers realised that belittlement, cynicism, sarcasm or any other behaviour that lessens an employee's sense of self will not generate more productivity or profits; quite the reverse. Happy workers not only are more creative and productive but are supportive of each other and of management, and this especially shows itself in times of crisis.

Not only do work organisations need to develop a culture of respect for workers, but they must also ensure that employees too respect each other, their employers and managers. Generally speaking, a circular reaction follows employers being respectful of employees or an employee being respectful of a colleague. In other words, what you provide for others is what you get back.

Nevertheless, there are individual workers, employers and managers who bring into the workplace the considerable emotional and cultural baggage of hating themselves and others, of aggression, of chronic dependence on others or on work performance, of hate of work or intolerable levels of work avoidance. The personal problems of any one person in an organisation cannot be allowed to violate the rights of others. Such neglect lowers the self-esteem of all concerned.

Workers, managers and employers have certain rights in common:

- ☐ The right to physical safety
- ☐ The right to sexual safety
- ☐ The right to emotional safety
- ☐ The right to intellectual safety
- ☐ The right to social safety
- ☐ The right to creative safety

The right to physical safety

There is no doubt but that there has been an improvement in physical safety in the workplace in terms of protective clothing, eye and ear protective devices, safer work environments and equipment. But some workplaces still fall short on hygienic toilet and wash-up facilities and clean and attractively designed canteens. And unfortunately, little progress has been made with regard to attacks on the physical integrity of workers (and indeed employers) that have devastating effects on self-esteem: pushing, bullying, spitting, violence, verbal threats, physical intimidation and put-down remarks on physical size, competence and appearance.

The more pleasing and safe a workplace is, the more workers receive the message: 'You are worthy of physical care.'

The right to sexual safety

The sexual boundaries of both men and women, but especially of women, have been and continue to be seriously violated. Every member of a work organisation has an inalienable right to sexual safety and should not experience any of the following:

- Verbal sexual harassment
- Gestural sexual harassment
- Uninvited touching or holding
- Sexual self-exposure
- Any physical interference of a sexual nature

The powerful message that the work organisation frequently needs to voice is 'Your right to sexual safety is recognised and any violation will be viewed seriously.' The work organisation needs to ensure that there is a safe, confidential forum for employees and managers to consult and that vindication of any violated rights is achieved through established structures.

The right to emotional safety

Whereas physical and sexual rights are now enshrined in the laws of most countries, emotional rights, which are equally essential to elevating people's self-esteem, have not yet attained such pro-tection. The most common attacks on the worthiness of workers and employers are emotional ones. The most sacred right of each person is to be loved and valued, and any behaviour that dimin-ishes that right is an emotional violation. Furthermore, the whole emotional world of employees needs to be respected. Employers need to realise that feelings are the most accurate barometer of what is happening to a worker at any one moment in time. An increase in emotional listening will certainly benefit employers and managers, especially males who have fought shy of most emotions, except anger. When a workplace does not create a safe atmosphere in which people can express fear, grievance, resentment, anger, joy, appreciation, insecurity, outrage, hurt or dismay, it means that a whole emotional underworld is created that can eventually rock the foundations of the organisation.

Apart from failure to value the person, threats to emotional integrity can take many other forms:

- Expressing outright rejection or hatred
- Mocking or laughing at a worker's fears
- Punishing emotion ('Don't be such a weakling', 'Real men don't cry')
- Diluting emotion ('You'll feel differently about it tomorrow', 'We all feel like that at times')
- Suppressing emotion ('You shouldn't feel resentful')
- Neutralising by demonstrating no recognition of emotion ('So what is it you want?', 'What's the problem?')

Acceptance, understanding and acting on feelings go the furthest towards ensuring that the self-worth of all members of the organisation is affirmed.

The right to intellectual safety

The right to respect for one's vast intellectual capacity is frequently violated in the workplace. Typically, most people confuse knowledge and skills with intelligence, and achievement and status within a company are often used as a means of feeling superior and making others feel inferior. But knowledge, competence and career status are only indices of learning and experience; they are not even remotely a measure of intelligence. As already stated, intelligence is a vast and unlimited potential to understand and adapt to the myriad of cultures we live in. The right to intellectual safety involves acknowledgment of this natural endowment and an acceptance of workers' present way of making sense and order of their world. Vindication of this right makes it possible for workers to accommodate further development of their unique potential. Any hint of criticism will simply serve to tighten their grip on how they currently function.

Threats to intellectual safety for employees, managers and employers can come in many ways:

- Ridiculing work efforts ('I've seen a child do better', 'You better pull up your socks')
- Being impatient and irritable with work efforts ('Jesus, hurry up man', 'This just won't do')
- Being intolerant and critical of mistakes and failures ('Failure is not a word used around here', 'Were you in outer space or what when you made that mistake?')
- Putting undue pressure on to succeed ('There is no excuse for not meeting targets', 'Failure is not accepted in here')
- Dismissing opinions ('What would you know about anything?', 'Who asked for your opinion?')
- Labelling ('You're thick', 'You're stupid', 'You're a lost cause', 'You're good for nothing')
- Criticising perceptions and means of doing things ('Where did that notion come from?', 'Just stick with what is asked of you')

What workers need to hear from managers and employers is an acknowledgment of their intelligence, a belief in their potential to learn, an acceptance of failure and success as integral to work and creativity, and an appreciation of their genuine efforts to achieve work targets.

The right to social safety

The social presence of every worker is a unique phenomenon and each has the right to acknowledgment of that specialness. In the workplace, people's right to social safety may be violated by:

- Ignoring their presence or absence
- Not addressing them by their preferred title
- Deliberately turning one's back on them
- Ostracising them
- Leaving them isolated
- Making snide comments about them
- Showing non-verbal hostility to their presence (acting in superior manner, looking down one's nose at them)
- Not including them in conversation
- Openly expressing irritability or aggressiveness towards them
- Making sarcastic comments ('Mr Perfect has just walked in', 'You don't have a clue what hard work means, do you Humphreys?')

There is no greater boost to a worker than to be told genuinely and sincerely, 'You are a special and valued member of this organisation.'

The right to creative safety

Our greatest needs as human beings are to be accepted for ourselves and to be free to live out our own unique existence. Being valued for self is the passport that permits us to be free to be ourselves.

Pressure to conform is the strongest block preventing workers from exercising their right to live their lives in their own unique and creative way. Forcing workers into behaviours that are contrary to their own beliefs and values is a gross infringement of their rights. Intolerance of differences in opinions and beliefs is yet another violation. The source of many problems in the workplace is that many workers are pushed into working against the grain of their own unique selves. The irony is that when workers are allowed the freedom to be themselves and to explore the world in their own unique and creative ways, they are far more productive, have greater job satisfaction and feel more self-fulfilled.

It is regrettable that many workers experience anonymity in the workplace. Work organisations need to ensure visibility and opportunities for real expression and creativity for their employees. It is the strong presence of workers that sets the scene for a dynamic workplace.

CARING WORK CULTURES

Workplaces do not have a history of being caring places, for either workers or managers. The caring work organisation has the philosophy that all who work under its umbrella are unique individuals with physical, sexual, emotional, intellectual, social, creative and spiritual rights and needs, and it does everything in its power to listen and to respond to these rights and needs. The caring work organisation knows that its person-centred approach will create the security, safety, challenge and excitement for all workers to take on the work goals of the organisation. It knows that valuing and affirming workers must always take precedence over productivity and profit. It accepts the profound influence that protective levels of self-esteem have on creativity, productivity and management. It engages in and fosters relationships that enhance workers' and managers' sense of themselves. It provides special attention to those who feel bad about themselves and lack self-confidence. It sees the specialness, worth and endless potential of these troubled workers and tries to communicate that image to them. It affirms the vast intellectual capacity of each of its workers and does not confuse knowledge or expertise with intellectual potential. It embraces failure and success as equal stepping-stones in the wonderful process of work and, especially, praises work efforts and a love of work. It seeks to make work and management enhancing of an employee's welfare. It knows the pitfalls in emphasising work performance, deadlines, and comparisons and competition with other companies. It puts particular stress on caring relationships between all members of staff and shows no tolerance of disrespect among employees or between managers and workers. It recognises the vulnerabilities of workers and managers and provides access to a confidential counselling service for them. It is concerned for those workers who either lost their love of work or never had a love of work and it offers opportunities for personal and professional growth and change. It recognises that its most valuable asset is its staff and it seeks to ensure that their work does not become more important than their worth.

Caring does not mean taking responsibility for people. What it does mean is creating a welfare environment wherein people learn to take self-responsibility and providing support and help for workers who are struggling.

Employees come into the workplace with a wide range of needs and if these are ignored, dismissed or neglected, their motivation to work and co-operate with job demands will be adversely affected. The caring work organisation reaches out with heart and mind to its members and does it in a way that does not jeopardise the work goals of the organisation. On the contrary, the mature organisation knows that everybody gains when workers feel cherished.

CHAPTER 9

MANAGEMENT, WORK AND WORTH

MANAGERS MANAGING THEMSELVES

If parents are the architects of the family culture, managers and employers are the major influence on the work culture. When a work organisation is multinational or has been in existence for some time, managers and supervisors will be selected to fit into the existing culture. Management style is indicative of the self-esteem of the manager and affects the self-esteem of workers, whether or not this fact is known by the individuals themselves or the work organisation. Furthermore, managers who subscribe to and reinforce work cultures that are neglectful of human welfare reflect their own troubled relationship with self and others.

It would appear that two main factors underlie management style: the maturity or emotional and cultural baggage of the managers, and the culture of the work organisation. As regards the latter factor, in many ways work organisations get the type of manager they deserve. When organisations are caring in nature they will be careful to select transformational managers and will keep a keen eye on management and staff relationships. However, when workplaces are not person friendly they tend to select managers who mirror such neglect.

Managers may come into their leadership role with addiction to work, or work may be a source of threat for them. Those addicted to work and aggressive in approach may express their need to prove themselves by high performance expectations, intolerance of mistakes and failures, highly critical reactions to work efforts, impatience, huge difficulties in delegating and an over-controlling and demanding management approach. Their sights will be set on productivity, and sensitivity towards the worth of self and employees will be absent. Their leadership style can be encapsulated in the saying 'Either shape up or ship out.'

Managers who demonstrate perfectionism and passivity tend to express their dependence on work by tremendously high expectations of self, high performance anxiety, non-voicing of expectations of workers, over-burdening of themselves, little delegation and hidden resentment towards others who do not work as hard as themselves.

The basis of effective management is for managers to manage themselves effectively. When managers lack control over their own personal, interpersonal and work lives they are not in a sufficiently mature position to be placed in charge of others

The following are some pertinent questions that managers need to ask of themselves:

- How do I regard myself?
- What adjectives would I use to describe myself?
- What adjectives would others use to describe me?
- Do I attempt to prove myself through work?
- Do I feel threatened by work?
- Would I describe myself as passive, aggressive, passive-aggressive or assertive?
- Do I have a balanced approach to work?

How do I regard myself?

This is a fundamental question. It has already been pointed out that men tend to dismiss the issues of self-worth, personal development, relationship enhancement, emotional literacy and the psychology of communication as 'only for women' or 'rubbish' or 'for sissies'. Such defensiveness does not augur well for male managers. Whether they like it or not, their concept of themselves will influence everything they do and be a considerable determining influence on how they lead others.

If you are a manager your first responsibility is to value yourself so that care of yourself is present before you attempt to care for and manage others. You need to recognise that the person most likely to neglect you is yourself. For instance, when you are aggressive towards yourself, or label yourself as a 'fool', 'weak' or 'stupid', or push yourself when tired, or miss meals, eat on the run, work long hours, or ridicule yourself, you are no longer creating a world wherein you are valued. You are now hardly in a position to request workers to be responsible and to care for themselves. Conversely, when you demonstrate self-possession and show good care of self, you are now in a strong position to request the same of others. Workers are quick to spot when managers have double standards and therein find justification to not respond to their requests.

It is quite extraordinary the number of managers who have no sense of their right to love, respect, nurturance and care of themselves. These deficits in self-care arise from a wider culture where children were reared to live their lives for others and punished for being themselves. This is regrettable, as the powerhouse of creativity, productivity and effective leadership is managers who act out from their uniqueness and limitless potential.

Actions that demonstrate respect for self are:

☐ Physical care of self
☐ Balanced lifestyle
☐ Listening to self
☐ Regular affirmation of own worth, uniqueness, vast capability and sacredness
☐ Valuing of and action on feelings
☐ Identification and vindication of own physical, sexual, emotional, intellectual, social, creative and spiritual rights
☐ Taking time for being with self
☐ Formation of and respect for own beliefs
☐ Encouragement and praise of own efforts at self-care
☐ Supporting self
☐ Challenging self

The self-regard activities least practised are taking time for being with self and challenging self. The capacity to enjoy your own company and the challenging of yourself to progress down the road of self-possession and spirituality are strong indices of maturity.

What adjectives would I use to describe myself?

The thoughts you have about self are mirrors of the protective level of your self-esteem. Typically, people are excellent at voicing protective adjectives but poor at voicing affirming ones. This is wise because the former have the power to reduce expectations while the latter carry the threat of increasing expectations. Unless you accept yourself for yourself you will engage in protective descriptions of yourself.

PROTECTIVE DESCRIPTIONS OF SELF

☐	Aggressive	☐	Inferior
☐	Anxious	☐	Intolerant
☐	Average	☐	Irritable
☐	Conservative	☐	Limited
☐	Daredevil	☐	Passive
☐	Dedicated	☐	Perfectionistic
☐	Depressed	☐	Radical
☐	Difficult	☐	Slow
☐	Dull	☐	Stupid
☐	Headstrong	☐	Superior
☐	Hesitant	☐	Timid
☐	Hyperactive	☐	Unapproachable

The possibilities are endless, but the ingenuity of each description must not be missed.

If you are fortunate enough to be in a place of deep regard for self and independent of others and work, your descriptions of yourself are more likely to be affirming of self.

AFFIRMING DESCRIPTIONS OF SELF

☐	Ambitious	☐	Empathic
☐	Assertive	☐	Energetic
☐	Balanced	☐	Equal
☐	Caring	☐	Fair
☐	Centred	☐	Firm
☐	Challenging	☐	Genuine
☐	Congruent	☐	Honest
☐	Confrontational	☐	Kind
☐	Conscientious	☐	Just
☐	Definite	☐	Level-headed

➔

- ☐ Non-possessive
- ☐ Open
- ☐ Private
- ☐ Responsible
- ☐ Spiritual
- ☐ Understanding
- ☐ Warm

Only about 5 to 10 per cent of adults will honestly describe themselves in these affirming ways.

What adjectives would others use to describe me?

This is a useful question to guard against self-delusion, which is a wonderful mechanism for not facing the challenge of truly evaluating how you perceive yourself. Ask the question of somebody you feel will be open and honest and who has known you for a long time. Sometimes it is a revelation to compare your list with that of your friend.

Do I attempt to prove myself through work?

This question was examined in chapter 3 and your reply to it will significantly affect how you manage. Your responsibility is to aim for a balanced approach to work (chapters 5 and 7) not only for your own welfare but also for the welfare of those workers for whom you have responsibility.

Do I feel threatened by work?

Chapters 3 and 4 teased out the manifestations of both the fear of work and the addiction to work, while the effects of these on leadership are discussed later in this chapter. From both an employer's and worker's point of view the manager who is threatened by work poses a greater threat than the one addicted to work.

Would I describe myself as passive, aggressive, passive-aggressive or assertive?

A true response to this question will reveal the type of leadership style you are likely to have adopted. Passive leadership results in a *laissez-faire* situation, aggressive leadership produces a rigid, controlled or rebellious workforce, while passive-aggressive leadership develops an uncertain work environment that is under mined by subterranean reactions on the part of workers. Only assertive leadership is likely to produce working relationships that are above board, honest, well-motivated and committed. It is crucial that managers who rate themselves as passive, aggressive or passive-aggressive address their protective forces as much for their own as for their charges' progress.

Do I have a balanced approach to work?

Workers and organisations can count themselves fortunate when managers are balanced. Such leaders have great influence, not only on people's work lives but also on their social, family, educational and spiritual lives.

The message here is that managers have a responsibility to address their own personal and cultural baggage before they take on the leadership of others. Work organisations and employers need to ensure they hire managers who are mature in their approach to work.

MANAGERS MANAGING OTHERS

Leaders are not born but are a product of remote and present influences and to what degree they have freed themselves of constrictive attitudes. The level of protection that managers have built around their own sense of self is a major determinant of how they interact with employees. Basically, managers cannot give what they have not got, so that if they do not feel good about themselves they cannot enable others to feel good about themselves. Of course, the opposite is true: managers with a strong sense of self can facilitate others to embrace their self-worth.

Because for those who possess a sense of inferiority work can be enmeshed with worth, it is inevitable that troubled managers will bring an unhealthy approach to the workplace, and managers who are addicted to or threatened by work will wreak havoc not only on their own personal, interpersonal and occupational life, but also on the lives of their workers. The more managers need to prove themselves through work, the more they will put pressure not only on themselves but also on employees. Managers who are addicted and also passive tend to put the greatest strain on themselves and will not directly request support and responsibility from workers. Leaders who are addicted and also aggressive will certainly push themselves, but they will also often make life hell for employees, with criticism and extreme demands. Neither type of manager is good at affirming self or employees.

Managers who are threatened by work and are aggressive tend to pass the buck of responsibility on to workers and demand a lot more of others than of themselves. They operate double standards and breed resentment in workers. Leaders who are threatened by work and are passive tend to bury their heads in the sand, hoping things will turn out all right and that difficulties will pass. There is no real leadership here and a state of 'anything goes' tends to operate.

Managers who have a balanced approach to work show mature care of themselves and are responsible and conscientious. They are good at affirming self and workers, and are direct and clear in their encouragement of workers' efforts and in confronting unacceptable work or interpersonal behaviours.

Managers have the important task of sorting out their own work and worth issues, but their organisation also needs to ensure there is appropriate management training. Management training often lacks a focus on personal development. Personal effectiveness lies at the heart of managerial effectiveness. Learning the skills of management does not ensure good leadership. Unless managers have achieved a fair degree of self-acceptance and independence of others' opinions and have broken the enmeshment of work and worth, they will not be in a safe enough place to risk practising effective management skills. The mature and balanced manager automatically engages in many of these so-called techniques of effective management. People are not stupid and they will employ the behaviours that best serve them (not necessarily the company) at any one moment.

Managers and workers' rights

The welfare and job satisfaction of workers must not be jeopardised by ineffective leadership. In other words, the personal problems of managers cannot be allowed to become violations of the rights of workers. These rights include:

- The right to physical, sexual, emotional, intellectual, social and creative safety (see chapter 8)
- The right to respect
- The right to work in a positive atmosphere
- The right to direct and clear communication
- The right to request help when required
- The right to fair and effective management
- The right to express any need or grievance
- When rights are violated, the right to have recourse to organisational structures that recognise, protect and vindicate those rights

These rights may appear fundamental, but, regrettably, there is substantial evidence that there are many workplaces in which they are not upheld.

The right to respect

Every worker is worthy of respect. It is the violation of this most basic right to respect that underlies many problems in the workplace. When workers themselves do not prioritise this right, they put themselves at great emotional, social and occupational risk. When the work organisation and its managers do not pay homage to this right and enshrine it in their policies, workers are at great risk.

The old belief that workers must earn respect from the manager is conditional in nature and implies that it is their actions and not their person that deserves respect. This is a recipe for conflict because workers are not their behaviour. Respect for another means honouring that person's unique being. There may be work and other behaviours that are unacceptable and that threaten or alienate managers, but these must be handled in a respectful way. Managers who do otherwise are engaging in the very behaviours they are condemning.

The right to work in a positive atmosphere

No worker should have to endure an atmosphere of hostility. Workers deserve to pursue their work goals without undue hindrance from colleagues or managers. It is often the case that a conscientious worker suffers hardship at the hands of less-motivated workers. It is poor management that does not detect and correct such bullying. Equally, the organisation fails everyone when it does not have mechanisms to reveal and resolve hostile or passive behaviours on the part of managers.

The right to direct and clear communication

Direct means that the message is addressed to the worker for whom it is intended and clear means that it is an 'I' message that is communicated. Consider the following communication from a manager to one of his workers: 'Michael, are you in a position to change shifts with John on Thursday? John needs some time off.' The difficulty with the 'you' message in this communication is that the manager is not owning his own need for Michael to cover a shift for John and, secondly, he is trying to get Michael to take responsibility for his need. The manager is entitled to make a request but not to pass the buck of responsibility on to the worker. In this example a direct and clear message would be: 'Michael, I'm stuck for somebody to cover John's shift and I would appreciate if you are in a position to swop with him.'

The right to request help when required

I know of so many workers who are terrified of seeking help when troubled or unsure or needing direction. Where this is so, it is likely that the type of management operating is oppressive in nature. Equally, I have talked to workers who do not make requests of managers or employers because they do not want to add to the pressure their leaders are already under. Such a situation suggests that the managers involved are addicted to work and take on far too many responsibilities. No matter what the reason, nobody gains when needs go unexpressed or difficulties are not challenged. Furthermore, in seeking aid there is openness about lack of competence or failure, and it is through this mature acceptance that there are opportunities to learn more effective work skills.

The right to fair and effective management

The level of personal security of managers and their attitudes towards workers have a profound effect on individual employees and on staff morale. Personal effectiveness is the foundation for professional effectiveness. When managers lack personal effectiveness they are likely to be aggressive, dogmatic and inflexible *or* passive, over-pleasing and indecisive *or* manipulative, cynical and defensive. Many workers complain that managers do not listen to, value or take action on their basic rights to physical, sexual, emotional, social, intellectual and creative safety. These workers speak of a lack of staff meetings, failure to recognise achievements, lack of opportunities to have an input into decision-making, unavailability and unapproachability of managers, and hostility to any attempt to confront ineffective management. Many workers experience outright abuse from managers. Clearly, none of this is acceptable, and workers themselves must band together to counter destructive leadership where it occurs. They need to assert strongly their right to fair and effective leadership and take firm action when such management is not forthcoming. Actions could include documenting violations of rights and needs, writing an operational policy and submitting it to all staff, management, the employer and the workers' union. Sometimes the radical action of 'downing tools' may be necessary to effect changes in leadership. Such confrontation is an act of caring, not only for the workers but also for the manager and the organisation. To ignore neglect is a rejection of self, and collusion with a manager's vulnerability only serves to perpetuate the problems. Confrontation, on the other hand, means that opportunities for progress are available for all.

The right to express any need or grievance

When the grievances of workers are not expressed they become a hidden underworld that shakes the organisation's effectiveness. Workers can become hostile, resentful, apathetic and clock-watching. Workers who have personal difficulty in voicing needs or grievances need to explore how they can support themselves or get support from others to resolve this passivity. When silence occurs because it is extremely unsafe to approach a manager, then recourse to back-up bodies is needed, for example higher management, the employer, unions, a solicitor or an ombudsman.

When rights are violated, the right to have recourse to organisational structures that recognise, protect and vindicate those rights

The creation of structures that protect and support the rights of workers is beginning to occur. Personnel departments, human resources management, employee assistance programmes and availability of confidential counselling are examples of such structures. Many workers still distrust these initiatives as being pro-management. Structures that arise from and include workers are more desirable and will be more readily accepted. Most workers still resort to trade unions. What is most important is that any such structure is seen to do its job effectively and justly.

Managing workers' needs

Managers carry difficult responsibilities for hiring, firing, confronting, setting targets, meeting deadlines, negotiating and mediating, but it is how they execute these tasks that matters most. Many complex and sophisticated models of management have been developed; these are often couched in jargon and sometimes are as confusing to managers as they are to workers. Effective management primarily concerns ensuring workers are articulate in expressing what they require of managers and vice versa.

It is not easy for managers when the most common language used by employees is the language of 'not tos'. Employees want leaders not to:

- ☐ Put them down
- ☐ Be aggressive
- ☐ Humiliate
- ☐ Denigrate
- ☐ Belittle
- ☐ Dismiss
- ☐ Publicly correct
- ☐ Be insensitive
- ☐ Be inconsiderate
- ☐ Be unfair
- ☐ Order
- ☐ Push and shove
- ☐ Sexually harass
- ☐ Physically harass
- ☐ Threaten
- ☐ Shout
- ☐ Be sarcastic
- ☐ Be cynical

It is more constructive and clear when needs are expressed positively. Workers need managers to:

- ☐ Be respectful
- ☐ Listen to their needs
- ☐ Be fair
- ☐ Be considerate
- ☐ Be open to differences of opinion
- ☐ Be sensitive
- ☐ Be approachable and available
- ☐ Correct positively
- ☐ Foster group decision-making
- ☐ Address workers by preferred title
- ☐ Recognise, appreciate and encourage work efficiency
- ☐ Be open to feedback on style of leadership
- ☐ Confront unacceptable behaviours
- ☐ Use 'I' messages
- ☐ Be direct and clear
- ☐ Hold regular staff meetings
- ☐ Be flexible
- ☐ Delegate responsibility fairly
- ☐ Be understanding
- ☐ Be firm
- ☐ Apologise for loss of control
- ☐ Apologise when mistaken
- ☐ When needed, seek help

Most of these needs speak for themselves. The demand for confrontation is a cry for clear communication on any personal, interpersonal or work issues that are a source of dissatisfaction to managers. As already outlined, progress at work is always best facilitated by honest, direct and open communication.

Because most people do not like to admit when they are wrong, genuine and sincere apologies for mistaken judgment or loss of control (for example aggression or public humiliation of a worker) are rare. But apologies are very important because they have the effect of healing the wound to a person's worth and the relationship between the conflicting parties, as well as creating a mature platform to resolve outstanding difficulties.

Managing staff morale

Because morale is the life-blood of the staff group, creating good morale is an important responsibility for managers. Morale is certainly boosted by attention to the self-worth of each employee, but it is also developed by frequent staff interactions (both occupational and social), group decision-making, staff affirmation by leaders, and leaders' availability and approachability. Approachable managers have the ability to make staff members feel sufficiently safe to come to them with work or other issues. Being available regularly at defined times and always in crises provides security for workers. Affirmation of workers is central to bringing about positive morale and yet it is the area most neglected in management. Affirmation involves finding the means to make all workers feel visible, not for what they do (that is praise) but for who they are. Even when workers are in touch with their self-worth, affirmation is a subtle, delicate issue, but when done well it has many rewarding consequences for workers and the work organisation. The following guidelines will help:

☐   *Only ever give honest and genuine affirmations.* If you are not genuine and do not really feel that the employee deserves the affirmation, your non-verbal language will give you away and the affirmation will be rejected as insincere.

☐ *Give an affirmation without expectation of a receptive response.* Generally, it is when a worker reacts defensively to an affirmation that that person most needs affirmation. You must not give up — an affirmation is an expression of something you feel and perceive and must not be given to gain a particular response.

☐ *The most powerful affirmation is undivided attention to the worker.* It is best to refrain from effusive compliments (they are rarely genuine). A look, a nod or a smile may be sufficient to affirm an employee. When in conversation with an employee be wary of being distracted by somebody else demanding attention. Only when you have fully completed your interaction do you allow yourself to attend to other demands.

☐ *Be sure the affirmation is unconditional and has no ulterior motive.* Do not give an affirmation to get something back (such as recognition in return, or a favour or praise) — that is manipulation and not affirmation.

☐ *Give affirmations frequently to create a mutual cycle of affirmation between members of staff.*

☐ *Avoid using clichés, jargon and popular superlatives (for example 'great!', 'super!', 'outstanding!', 'A1!').* Use language that is down to earth and real and that comes from the heart.

☐ *Spontaneous unconditional affirmations are the most powerful.*

It is important not to confuse affirmation with praise. There are many actions of workers that deserve praise, reward and recognition. However, it is for their unique person that workers want recognition, and this is what affirmation is all about. Examples of affirmations include acknowledging workers' presence and absence, demonstrating affection, calling workers by their preferred title, showing concern when absent or sick or seemingly off form, listening when being addressed and making positive eye contact.

Most workers will respond in kind to managers who genuinely make efforts to meet their needs. A minority of employees have severe problems in living and working, and managers will need powerful back-up support from the work organisation and trade unions to counter their destructive effects. Trade unions which countenance the non-sanctioning or continued employment of such workers do no service to their own organisation, to the workers themselves, to other employees whose rights are often jeopardised and to the employing organisation. Equally, there is a sizeable number of managers who are highly vulnerable and who, as a result, can cause great hardship to employees. Work organisations, unions and employees themselves must not tolerate such staff relationships.

MANAGERS AND THE ORGANISATION

The work organisation must always be more powerful than the manager. It is its responsibility not only to be the watchguard of managers' functioning but also to select managers who have at heart the welfare of themselves, the workers and the organisation. It is also the role of the organisation to back the positive policies and actions of managers. Many managers are left isolated in their difficult role and are often under siege from workers who perceive this weakness in the organisation.

Selection of managers is not a matter to be taken lightly. Even a responsible, creative and highly skilled work record does not guarantee mature management. Management goes beyond work knowledge and skills to knowing how to relate to, motivate and understand workers and how to obtain loyalty and commitment from them. To do this, it requires the foundation of a strong acceptance of self, independence of others, and separateness from and a balanced attitude towards work.

When hiring managers the selection panel need to discover the applicants' basic concept of management. They need to know whether potential candidates view managing as a matter of:

- Over-powering or empowering
- Protecting or empowering
- Being passive or active
- Being rigid or flexible
- Being uncaring or caring
- Being profit focused or people focused
- Being conditional or unconditional
- Being neutral or empathic
- Being incongruent or congruent

When a manager's basic belief is to over-power, the organisation needs to understand that not only is such a style of management a violation of workers' self-worth, but it also stores up major difficulties for the organisation. Workers who conform and yield to a manager's dominating behaviour develop a wide range of self-esteem protectors that limit both their personal and their work effectiveness·

Anxiety	Fear of seeking help when needed
Criticism of self	
Dependence	Lack of initiative
Fear of change	Loss of ambition
Fear of mistakes and failures	Neglect of physical welfare
Fear of rejection	Perfectionism

- Sense of inferiority
- Sensitivity to criticism
- Shame
- Susceptibility to hurt
- Tendency to please people
- Tendency to live in the future
- Unhappiness

An over-powering style of management can also engender rebellious responses which create much conflict and unhappiness in the
workplace. As with conformist responses, rebelliousness is a
defensive means to offset hurt and humiliation. With rebelliousness the very behaviours of the over-powering managers are what
they get in return. Typical rebellious behaviours are:

- Absenteeism
- Aggression
- Arrogance
- Carelessness
- Control of others
- Creation of like-minded cliques
- Cynicism
- Hatred of work
- Hostile sense of humour
- Hostility
- Low ambition
- Low initiative
- Low productivity
- Manipulation
- No commitment
- Sarcasm
- Superiority complex
- Temper tantrums
- Unco-operativeness
- Violence
- Vocal on own rights

The more intense, enduring and frequent are the over-powering
behaviours of managers, the greater the defences of workers.
Organisations may attempt to justify neglectful practices by saying
that workers are responsible for themselves and that it is they
who are to blame if they choose to put up with a dominating
management style. It is the case that workers who are balanced
will not tolerate such neglectful management, but many workers
are not in such a mature position. Organisations have responsibilities towards workers and passing the buck is a defensive action
which can be neither justified nor tolerated.

Whilst workers who are over-powered by management develop a host of defensive reactions that are detrimental to work organisations, a protective management style can be equally problematic. Males tend towards dominance and females towards protection in their style of management. Neither approach is beneficial to workers or employers. Responses to protectiveness can also be either conformist or rebellious. Workers who conform accept the manager's doing everything for them and they suitably show:

□ Cautiousness	□ Neediness
□ Dependence	□ Passivity
□ Fearfulness	□ Poor initiative
□ Fear of change	□ Sensitivity to criticism
□ Helplessness	□ Sulkiness
□ Hostile silences	□ Timidity
□ Indecisiveness	□ Unadventurousness
□ Lack of ambition	□ Unsureness
□ Lack of autonomy	

Workers who conform to an over-protective style of management are likely to have experienced similar over-protection in their family of origin. It is a difficult task for these workers to understand the implicit demand to be helpless. To show power in homes, schools and work cultures that are protective in nature would mean risking rejection. Conformity becomes a clever means of preventing such a devastating occurrence. These workers are not weak; on the contrary, they have found powerful ways of protecting themselves from being abandoned.

Employees who rebel against the over-protective manager do so to reduce the threat of being emotionally smothered. Such a manager does not truly value the unique person and vast capability of workers; indeed this manager's ways are constant threats to their self-worth. Rebelliousness indicates a worker's dependence on acceptance by authority figures; it is not a bid for freedom as some people think, but a bid to reduce hurt. Rebellious reaction to protection can take many forms:

- Aggression
- Constant need to prove self
- Daredevil behaviour
- Denial of problems
- Difficulty in seeking support or help
- Hostile sense of humour
- Intolerance
- Irritability
- Isolation from others
- Moodiness
- Neglectful of physical welfare
- Over-ambition
- Pseudo-independence
- Superiority complex
- Threatened by opposition
- Troubled relationships with other workers

Managers who adopt either an over-powering or a protective approach are also typically rigid and conditional. Those who dominate expect adherence to their beliefs and ways, and those who protect want workers to remain dependent and helpless. The conditionality in both practices is reflected in the fact that any deviation from expectations results in some form of rejection of the worker. The rejection could take the form of rage, 'put downs', ostracisation or hostile silences. Whilst both these types of leaders can show caring for workers, their caring is not unconditional but rather manipulative. In other words, these managers are saying 'Once you do as I say, want and need, I will value you.' Dominant leaders tend to be profit focused and those who are protective more people focused, but due to the conditional nature of the relationship, there is a pseudo aspect to their being person focused. Only leaders who are balanced are truly congruent, caring and empathic. Again it may seem that managers who are protective are empathic, but subconsciously, they are more concerned with how they feel themselves.

There are managers who are passive in their roles and allow employees too much power. These managers lack confidence, have highly protected self-esteem, are fearful and are easily threatened by conflict and failure. Their lack of leadership creates chaos, insecurity for workers and a working environment where the conscientious employee may become apathetic and where those who are rebellious and avoid work run riot.

Mature managers are active, empowering, flexible, caring, person centred, unconditional, empathic and congruent in their pursuit of organisational goals. The real test of leadership is the relationship that managers create with workers. Many managers require training in a management style that is caring and transformational in nature. This kind of management is based on the belief that responsible leaders can empower employees and foster a work life that is meaningful and satisfying for all.

Transformational management creates a work environment based on a number of clear principles.

PRINCIPLES OF TRANSFORMATIONAL MANAGEMENT

- Workers have immense potential and given the right circumstances will work hard to apply it.
- Workers deserve to be treated with respect and dignity.
- Workers understand the purpose of their work and the goals of the organisation.
- All members of the work organisation are accountable.
- Managers and workers are able to identify and learn from mistakes and problems before they escalate or are transferred to higher levels of the organisation.

→

- ☐ Employers and managers are responsible for acquainting workers with the working of the organisation.
- ☐ Managers are responsible for ensuring that skills and information are shared and communicated in a two-way process.
- ☐ Employers, managers and workers have a responsibility to each other. This responsibility translates into a sense of respect, empathy, understanding, caring and mutual support.

Transformational management creates a workplace where managers and workers believe in and care about their work. It provides challenges by emphasising solutions to problems and it encourages individual growth, self-knowledge, and occupational, physical, social and spiritual enhancement. Employers and managers who practise this philosophy lead with both the head and the heart.

Effective managers possess:

- ☐ A clear vision of how they want the workplace to be
- ☐ The ability to communicate this vision and gain the support of workers
- ☐ Persistence, consistency and focus, particularly when workers show a lack of responsibility
- ☐ The capacity to empower employees to work towards their individual and collective goals; the emphasis is on self-responsibility, questioning and altering limiting beliefs, and the development of a sense of spiritual self
- ☐ The capacity to use innovative ideas and practices that enable the organisation to monitor its progress — past and present — and its overall effectiveness

Transformational managers are perpetual learners who mature from their own and others' experiences. Effective managers know that self-worth and a joy of learning are the mainsprings of effectiveness, sources of energy that maintain a love of work by continually triggering new understanding, new ideas and new challenges.

Workers who are victims of ineffective managers would do well to seek out ways of empowering themselves and to ally themselves with colleagues who are unwilling to yield to the untenable situation.

PART IV

STARTPOINT

'It's a joy to remain hidden but a disaster not to be found.'

D.W. Winnicott

CHAPTER 10

PREVENTING THE ENMESHMENT OF WORK AND WORTH

BEING TWO STEPS AHEAD

There is today a great need to focus on restoring that wonderful eagerness to learn that is innate to infants but has been extinguished in so many adults. However, it needs to be seen that a much greater loss precedes the extinguishing of the eagerness to learn; this is the loss of love for our sacred, unique and vastly capable selves. These two losses — the loss of love for self and the loss of love for learning — point to the two steps required to prevent the enmeshment of work and worth. The first step is for those in positions of leadership (parents, teachers, employers, managers) to create unconditional relationships with self and with others. The second step is to ensure that work and learning environments pose no threat to the desire to learn.

Loss of love creates massive insecurity, and where the loss is accompanied by harshness, criticism, physical punishment, irritability, dismissiveness, cruelty or sexual abuse the consequences are hopelessness, despair, unrelenting internal grief, rage and great anxiety. The experience is equivalent to 'soul' murder, and considerable long-term help and love are required to redeem people from the terrible darkness of not being cherished. The physical, social, emotional and spiritual consequences of loss of love vary in accordance with the extent of the loss. Those who have had to hide the precious and unique pearl of self from those who are in shadow will do anything to stop the deepening of invisibility. Conformity to the expectations of the significant adults in our lives is one powerful way of ensuring less anonymity. Even though we unconsciously know that such conformity does not gain unconditional love, it at least merits recognition for the expected behaviours and keeps open the possibility of finding true love.

The behaviours required in order to merit recognition may be emotional, social, religious, occupational, intellectual, physical, sexual or domestic. Typical examples are:

□   *Emotional*
- 'If you care for me then I will love you.'
- 'If you show no weaknesses then I will have regard for you.'

□   *Social*
- 'If you impress others with your accomplishments then I will see you.'
- 'If you let me down in front of others then I will reject you.'

□   *Religious*
- 'If you are a good Catholic I will love you.'
- 'If you marry someone who is not of our religion I will have nothing to do with you and your partner.'

□   *Occupational*
- 'If you become a doctor we will feel proud of you.'
- 'If you are successful we will love you.'

□   *Intellectual*
- 'If you are clever academically we will be so proud.'
- 'If you perform highly in your examinations we will value you.'

☐   *Physical*
- 'If you keep yourself clean and spotless I will be so pleased with you.'
- 'If you are beautiful I will want you.'

☐   *Sexual*
- 'If you satisfy me sexually I will love you.'
- 'If you show no sexual longings I will stay close to you.'

☐   *Domestic*
- 'If you keep everything clean and tidy you will be special to me.'
- 'If you allow me to do everything for you I will never leave you.'

Children and adults know full well the consequences of not living up to the conditions of love. A father once told me of how he so much wanted his first son to be perfect so that he would become visible to others. Sadly, every time the child fell short of his unrealistic expectations he was critical and irritable and sometimes physically punishing and dismissive of his child. He also found himself constantly monitoring his child's behaviour both in and out of home. By the age of eleven the boy showed nervous tics, excessive eye blinking, avoidance of adults, hatred of school work and a need to be always with his peer group. Of course, this father did not want to make his son highly insecure, but his own sense of invisibility led him to project his need for recognition on to his child. While eschewing judgment, nonetheless those of us who find ourselves projecting our own difficulties on to others have a responsibility to look to ourselves, to love and respect others for themselves and not for what they do, and to create positive learning and work environments.

It is not difficult to notice when we adversely affect the lives of others; the fall-out of our behaviour is designed to wake us up to our own vulnerabilities and to the threats we pose to others and to push us to find the help and support we need to resolve both our inner and our outer conflicts. Possible reactions from others include:

□	Absenteeism	□	Lack of communication
□	Aggression	□	Lack of initiative
□	Avoidance of contact	□	Low motivation
□	Conformity	□	Perfectionism
□	Eagerness to please	□	Physical illness
□	Fearfulness	□	Timidity

The more intense and enduring the reaction, the more urgent is the need for change both for the person who displays and for the person who experiences the threatening behaviour.

The second step is to ensure that learning and work environments pose no threats to people's natural curiosity and eagerness to learn. This is a vital step and a difficult one in a society where work, success and wealth are so highly valued. Unless we move away from the hollowness of materialism we will continue to put at risk people's emotional, social and spiritual welfare and, ironically, also limit productivity and creativity.

Efforts at prevention need to take place in all the key social systems that children and adults inhabit: the home, the school and the workplace.

PREVENTION IN THE HOME

There are few parents who do not carry some degree of emotional baggage into their role as family leader. The greater their unresolved conflicts, the more parents will adversely affect the overall development of their children. Parents, who are the architects of the family, must look to themselves and analyse how they relate to self and their children and how they approach work, learning and teaching. Some questions that parents need to ask themselves are: 'Am I performance driven?' and 'How do I respond to failure and success?'

It can be difficult to stand back and examine how you view work. It can sometimes help to get feedback from someone who is in a place to give an honest evaluation, someone who is mature, balanced, objective and compassionate. Basically, what you are attempting to discover is how much of a friend you are to yourself. A friend is affectionate, warm, caring, gentle, encouraging, affirming, supportive, understanding, compassionate, firm and challenging; a friend listens to you, has belief in your vast capability and helps you to learn from mistakes and not be seduced by success. The deficits you discover in your friendship with yourself you will also see in your relationship with your children. In correcting how you are with yourself, you take the first step in preventing your children from losing their sense of their sacred selves.

When parents enmesh worth and work, this inevitably will be projected on to children. Work can be a wonderful pleasure; when it is not, parents need to examine seriously what has gone wrong and see how what has been lost can be restored. Cutting the ties that bind worth to work entails parents embracing their unique selves and not allowing any behaviour, work or otherwise, to shadow the light of their unique being. It also includes putting work in perspective, as only one of the many important aspects of living, along with relationships, spirituality, education, creativity, recreation, and physical, emotional and social well-being. When parents love work, stay separate from it and keep it in perspective, they offer their children an environment where their natural love of learning, and later on work, will flourish.

These responsibilities are an essential part of parenting; failure to fulfil them continues the cycle of enmeshment of work and worth and its catastrophic consequences.

Love children for themselves, not for what they do

Unconditional love — loving children for themselves, not for what they do — is the *sine qua non* of effective parenting; it also guarantees that when these children become adults they will not enmesh work and worth. Because unconditional love has tended to be a rare phenomenon few people are secure emotionally, socially, spiritually and occupationally. However, a new era is dawning where it is beginning to be seen how essential and how powerful is unconditional regard for self, for children and for others. Where there is unconditional love there is no confusion of behaviour with person. At times there will be behaviours that are difficult and perhaps even threatening; but if you are confronted with difficult behaviour it is important that your respect for the person and for yourself does not weaken. This does not mean you turn a blind eye to the problem behaviour. On the contrary, you remain definite and determined that such behaviour will not be tolerated and will not in any way be allowed to diminish your worth. But how you confront is a crucial issue. You are much more likely to get a positive response when you focus on unacceptable behaviour rather than judge the person.

For example, if I say to my child 'Michael, you're a bold boy and you shouldn't be hitting your brother', Michael's back is now against the wall, he will feel rejected by me and his only recourse is to fight back or sullenly withdraw. Either way, the relationship between us has become strained and considerable effort may be needed to restore it to a state of welfare. I am more likely to resolve the problem if I say 'Michael, I will not accept you hitting your brother and I am requesting you to not do it again. I want you to learn to resolve your difficulties in a respectful way.' Generally speaking, parents are not good at apologising to children and this can result in a deepening of the rift between them.

A great index of an unhappy family is the absence of apologies. This index can be applied equally to the school, workplace or community.

Many people struggle with the practice of unconditional love; this is not surprising, as most of us were reared on the opposite. As a result, we protectively became convinced that we are our behaviour and that our worth lies in what we do and not in what we are. Each person is unique, sacred, unrepeatable, wonderful, beautiful and vastly capable. Before the first bit of behaviour you ever exhibited, all that you are was present, and it is still present even though it may be hidden in the dark shadows of insecurity, doubt or despair. No behaviour either adds to or takes away from your person. Behaviour is your way of experiencing the world. 'I am not my behaviour' needs to be shouted from the rooftops of all homes, schools and workplaces. We all need to proclaim: 'Please love me for myself. Encourage, correct and guide my behaviour but do not entangle my person with any bit of behaviour.'

Embrace equally failure and success

Being able to embrace equally failure and success is the cornerstone of preventing the loss of love of work. Western culture has lost the sense of the importance, necessity, power and creativity of failure and its vital connection to effective learning. We tend to respond to success as if it were the end of all endeavour and to punish and ridicule failure. Furthermore, society has personalised success and failure by acclaiming successful people and denigrating those seen as failures. There is no such phenomenon as a successful person or a failure of a person; in any one day each person has a mixture of success and failure experiences. Failure and success are interwoven phenomena in the art of learning. Every failure spells out what has been learned and signposts what now needs to be adjusted, revised, added to or discontinued; its occurrence, rather than being a reason for criticism and punishment, must be greeted as an opportunity for further learning. This honouring of failure is brought out in the story of the person who said to Thomas Edison that, since he had two thousand failures at making a light bulb, wasn't it time he gave up his ambition, to which Edison (who incidentally had been regarded as a dunce in school) responded: 'No, I now know of two thousand ways of how not to make a light bulb!'

Parents too need to evaluate their response to success. My stomach turns when I see parents being overjoyed with success and showing overt disappointment when success eludes either themselves or their children. Learning is what needs to be celebrated most of all, and learning is always present whether the experience is one of success or failure. To treat success differently from failure is to break the vital link between them. A success-driven culture makes learning and work such difficult challenges. A focus on success means always having to maintain a high standard, and this pressure often results in people avoiding learning and work challenges.

Success needs to be received in the same way as failure; both are integral to learning and work. A positive reception to their presence will ensure learning and work remain worthwhile and exciting challenges.

What counts is effort

If failure and success form the engine of learning, then effort is the fuel that drives it. Many parents, teachers and managers attempt to make learning and work performance driven, but the result is an engine that burns out or stalls or comes to a complete standstill. Performance anxiety accounts for so much dried up or exhausted potential. Parents who emphasise and praise efforts to learn rather than performance are to the forefront in preventing learning and work becoming threatening experiences.

Parents must evaluate whether or not their own approach to work is performance driven. This is not difficult to do: our words, thoughts and actions constantly betray our dependence on performance:

- □ 'I never get anything right.'
- □ 'Winning is what counts.'
- □ 'If you can't do something right then don't do it at all.'
- □ 'I can't bear not to win.'
- □ 'I'll avoid a challenge when there is a threat somebody else will surpass me.'
- □ 'A pass examination result means nothing to me.'
- □ 'When I'm not successful at an interview I see myself as a failure.'

It may help parents to take the risk of letting go of having to be successful to realise that, when they make effort to learn and work their target, they focus all their energy on the task in hand, rather than splitting it between anxiety to succeed and work concentration. Learning and productivity are considerably enhanced by valuing effort, and there are no limiting consequences as there are for lauding performance. The most important responsibility for parents is to perpetuate children's natural love of learning and work. When parents themselves (and teachers and other leaders) are not performance driven they can see clearly that learning and work are best served by encouraging and praising effort.

Parents, teachers and employers often complain to me that children or workers are 'just plain lazy'. The human psyche is never lazy, but it can create an image of apathy and laziness to offset threats to self. Laziness is the shadow behaviour that protects the eagerness to learn and work which has become too threatened to show itself in an environment where performance is a measure of a person's worth and work. Judgments, criticism and harassment only serve to harden the protective crust. Protection will continue until those who judge look at their own approach to work and then at how they approach the work efforts of others. Parents, teachers, managers and employers need to practise what they preach; otherwise, their demands will fall on deaf ears.

PREVENTION IN THE SCHOOL

Like parents, teachers first need to examine their own relationship with themselves, the degree of enmeshment of work with their sense of self, the nature of their relationship with students, their responses to failure and success, and the extent to which they value effort above all else in teaching children. Difficulties around any of these issues will produce similar difficulties in their students.

The teacher has further responsibilities over and above those shared with parents. The key issues revolve around the school's phil-osophy of education, its view of students and how teaching is done.

How the school views education

Regrettably, many schools have got trapped into an education system that is driven by examination performance rather than a love of learning. Pressures from parents, school managers, employers and government departments have undermined the joy in teaching for many teachers and their desire to educate children for all aspects of living. More than any other profession, teachers are publicly evaluated in terms of results. Ironically, the best teaching is not always achieved with those students who attain

As and Bs (they are well motivated anyway, though not always maturely so), but with those students who fear learning and who come to school with less knowledge than their more advantaged peers. Today there is some recognition of this and resources are now being made available to those students who come from less privileged circumstances. What is still not being recognised is that the potential of these students is equal to that of those who are considered advantaged, but more work is required to bring them up to a par on knowledge and skills.

Schools that see their role as preparing students for examination may achieve high academic results, but there may be emotional, social, recreational and spiritual deficits in both teachers and students. Schools that are geared towards the holistic development of students can rest assured that their students will hold fond memories of their school years. My prediction is if research compared these two types of schools, on academic results alone, the holistic school would fare better. It is difficult to find a sufficient number of such schools to make the comparison.

Prevention of work and worth problems can be achieved in schools with a philosophy that is student centred, that recognises the unique ways and contribution of each student and that sees education as being not just about the accumulation of knowledge but about the overall development of the student.

How teachers view students

Whether in the home, school or workplace, relationships are the key to people's healthy development and the only mature relationship is the unconditional one. Teachers who have conditional ways of relating to children, or who have come to a place of not caring, pile up problems around worth and work for themselves and their students. But such neglect is frequently left unconfronted. The school that is determined to prevent such problems will have built-in safeguards against the development of blocking processes. Its mission statement will celebrate the sacredness and uniqueness of each student and teacher and will not tolerate disrespect of any member. The school will also affirm the vast intellectual potential of all members and will not confuse intelligence with knowledge. It will avoid labelling students as 'weak' or 'average' or 'good'. It will value all expressions of being and not just academic learning. It will avoid competition between students and will encourage self-competition. It will want each student to feel wanted and to love and enjoy learning. It will offer compassion, concern and effective help to those students whose eagerness to learn has already a protective crust around it. No judgment will mar its caring, and this caring will be done in such a way that the person and rights of others are not jeopardised.

How teachers teach

The 'what' of teaching has been over-emphasised to the detriment of the 'how' of teaching. Learning needs to be exciting, challenging and always non-threatening. Teachers who instruct with passion and joy do not make learning something to fear, abhor or be bored with, but make it the positive experience that children deserve it to be. Regrettably, school can be a mixed blessing for children. Some teachers are excellent in their relationships with students and in the positive learning atmosphere they create; others instil fear and dread; still others pose unrealistic expectations; and finally there are a small number who have become apathetic and fail to inspire students to maintain their love of learning.

Schools need to monitor the learning environment of each classroom to ensure a poor learning ethos does not threaten children's worth and learning. Such a monitoring system is not designed to be a watchguard on teachers; on the contrary, teachers who create difficult classroom environments need help as much as the students they are teaching. The aim is to have a school wherein the worth of each member is recognised and celebrated and where work is a joy for all.

PREVENTION IN THE WORKPLACE

Many workers experience the workplace as a prison wherein they feel anonymous and where there is no release for emotion and creativity. Where such an ethos exists employees wake up in the morning dreading the day. There is no doubt that certain work-places or work can darken human presence. Workers feel that their contribution is merely functional and rarely appreciated. Such a workplace blocks personal growth and creativity and creates major difficulties around personal worth and work.

While the ethos of a workplace is a complex and subtle group presence, it has a powerful effect on all those who enter its doors. If employers want to prevent work and worth problems, they need to set about creating an atmosphere that is respectful and celebratory of individuality, is happy, caring and kind, and welcomes emotional expression and creativity. Where the work atmosphere is life-giving, wonderful things can occur. It is a joy to come to work, to have a feeling of belonging and dignity. An enriching and dynamic flow can then exist between employees' homes, private worlds and work.

As for homes and schools, how employers and managers view themselves, others, relationships, success and failure, learning and the development of knowledge and skills is the essential determinant of the work ethos. What has been outlined for homes and schools on these matters applies equally and powerfully to the workplace.

How employers view workers

When the individuality and unique contribution of each worker are not seen in the workplace this absence becomes a dark breeding ground for work and worth problems. Employers and managers, even where there are large workforces, have to find ways of individualising workers. The achievement of this will be largely determined by whether or not employers and managers possess genuine respect for themselves. I say 'genuine' because there are leaders who have a superior view of themselves but an inferior regard for employees. Genuine regard for others automatically equalises relationships. A major preventative initiative would be for work organisations to have their leaders undergo an evaluation of how they are in relationship to themselves, others and work. Resolution of difficulties in these spheres would reduce the level of projection from leaders on to workers. It is important that any opportunity to reflect on self, others and work is provided in a safe, non-judgmental and dynamic way and by people who are suitably qualified. This process could be organised at either a group or individual level. For employers and managers who are in the deep shadows of self-doubt, alienation from others (through either aggression or passivity) and addiction to or avoidance of work, a confidential one-to-one therapeutic consultancy is required. The organisation itself must show clear support for its leaders to be mature and respectful of others and have a balanced approach to work. Such endorsement would need to be in the company's mission statement and concretised in operational and personnel policies.

Another preventative action that a workplace could take is periodic examination of its culture. The assessor would need to have knowledge and experience of work cultures but, even more importantly, would need to have the skills to observe the workplace with a divergent and imaginative eye. The result of such an analysis is more likely to be engaging and inspirational for both leaders and employees than an analysis that is bogged down by a purely functional approach and jargonistic language. The aim is to release the energies, creativity, individuality and unique contributions of all within an atmosphere of mutual respect between all members of the work organisation.

How the organisation views work

When work serves only the work organisation, there is a major deficit within the work culture. Work also needs to serve the workers, especially in terms of fair wages, worthy working conditions, being person, relationship and family friendly, and being a source of social get-togethers. Where possible a share in profits considerably boosts morale. Organisations need also to extend their benefaction to the community, not just with money but by involvement in projects (for example sports, health, tidy towns, creative initiatives that enhance the community image and lend assistance to people who are disadvantaged). The more that workers see the organisation as having an expansive view of work, the more they will be honoured to be numbered among its ranks, thereby leading to a lessening of work and worth problems. What work organisations must guard against is workers being reduced to a function. This is literally soul-destroying and will prove counter-productive in the long run. People must always count more than product.

Prevention of worth and work problems is also aided by workplaces being concerned about and actively arranging both short- and long-term education of employees; this need not necessarily be geared towards career development. Such involvement will certainly make workers feel valued, and it could have the added advantage of workers remaining loyal to the organisation. Many employers struggle with high staff turnover, and the present healthy economic climate makes employee movement more likely. Workshops, seminars, lectures and literature for both management and staff on the positive nature of work, staff relationships, communication, time management, personal empowerment, leadership, stress management, self-esteem and balanced lifestyle could considerably benefit individuals and the work culture.

Work organisations need to hold on to the principle that mature and contented workers are the backbone of efficient and effective work output. There has to be a 'walk talk' reality to such a belief; those organisations that pretend allegiance will not reap the rewards of satisfied employees working joyfully, efficiently and effectively. Employers also need to be prepared for employees' scepticism when they implement person-centred management; persistence in genuine and sincere practice will dissolve workers' protective fears.